DATE DUE

Clarence Darrow: Public Advocate

Designed by Bob Bingenheimer

Edited for production by University
Publications editorial staff

Typeset in Palatino Roman on the Mergenthaler
V-I-P phototypesetter by the University
Publications composition department

Printed for Wright State University by
the Horstman Printing Co., Dayton, Ohio

Clarence Darrow: Public Advocate

by James Edward Sayer

Monograph Series Number 2
Wright State University
Dayton, Ohio

Library of Congress Catalog Card Number 78-51212

The Wright State University Monograph Series was established for the purpose of publishing works of distinctive merit, mainly by members of the Wright State University faculty. These works are to be the results of significant research in any discipline, considered by experts to be of value to specialists and, on occasion, to the public at large. Creative works may also be included in the series.

This second volume in the University Monograph Series examines Clarence Darrow not as a lawyer, about which much has already been written, but as a master rhetorician who through his public debates has profoundly influenced both the style and the content of American thought.

University Monograph Committee:

Donald R. Swanson, Chairman and Editor
Robert Dolphin, Jr.
Jacob Dorn
R. Fred Rolsten
Robert S. Topor

Foreword

It is both a pleasure and an honor to write this introduction to the second publication in the Wright State University Monograph Series. There is no doubt that this outlet provides an opportunity for our faculty, and the present monograph is a case in point.

Professor Sayer has chosen a subject in which his attention is focused on a somewhat ignored area in the career of one of America's most exciting and controversial trial attorneys. For anyone interested in debate, as Professor Sayer is, Clarence Darrow cannot help but prove attractive. He was controversial, opinionated, and apparently incapable of taking the middle ground, as is true of most successful trial attorneys.

Clarence Darrow identified strongly with one side or the other. He was not given to calm, judicious analysis. For him, once the battle was drawn, he was totally immersed and almost incapable of even desiring to see his opponent's position. This attitude makes for excitement, strong judgments, and sensationalism. Clarence Darrow was all of these, and I am sure that this monograph, which concentrates on his public debates, will be a valuable contribution to the controversies which still surround Clarence Darrow. This will be an important addition to the University's Monograph series.

Andrew P. Spiegel
Executive Vice-President and Provost

Acknowledgments

I should like to acknowledge the following individuals who made this monograph a reality: Professor Raymond Yeager of Bowling Green State University, who provided the initial impetus for this study; Professor Donald Swanson, the University Monograph Committee, and the University Publications department of Wright State University, who edited, encouraged, and produced this final volume; and Cathy, who had to endure her husband's alter ego, Clarence Darrow.

J.E.S.

Contents

Chapter One

Clarence Darrow: Advocate

By the time of his death in 1938, Clarence Seward Darrow had become an imposing figure of national stature. Active in legal, political, and social contests, Darrow had become a living "myth" in his own time.[1] Very few people in the United States did not know his name or face, and his many celebrated public causes had made him an important "segment of the national conscience" during the 1920s and 1930s.[2]

Born near Kinsman, Ohio, in 1857, Darrow had a minimum of formal education before attending Allegheny College in Meadville, Pennsylvania. The Panic of 1873 destroyed the meager Darrow family financial resources and Clarence was forced, after but one year in college, to return home to take a job. After serving as a public school teacher for three years, he decided upon a legal career and, at the age of twenty, entered studies at the University of Michigan School of Law. However, Darrow did not enjoy his year of academic study and decided not to return for more formal education. Instead, he secured a clerk's job in a law office in Youngstown, Ohio, and spent his spare hours reading various books until his admission to the bar in 1878.

After nine years of practice in small Ohio towns, Darrow moved to Chicago in 1887. Within the next seven years he held the posts of special assessment attorney, assistant corporation counsel, corporation counsel and head of the law department for the city of Chicago, and general attorney for the Chicago and North Western Railway Company. Throughout this time, Darrow had become prominent in city politics and had also become an important leader in Henry George's single tax movement—a plan to streamline the nation's economy for the supposed betterment of the middle and lower classes. By 1894, it appeared that Clarence Darrow was about to carve an important niche for himself in the practice of corporate law. He had been extremely successful in representing his employers against claims lodged by various labor groups, and he was greatly admired and respected by the big business interests in the Chicago area.

However, when Eugene V. Debs and his American Railway Union were charged with criminal conspiracy in the formulation and prosecution of the Pullman Strike in 1894, Darrow resigned his railway position to defend the great labor leader. He offered a simple explanation for this decision: "I believe in the right of the people to better themselves, and I'm going to throw in my ten cents' worth to help them."[3] This decision marked the end of Darrow's civil claims practice and began his career as the paramount labor attorney in conspiracy and injunction suits. His successful defense of Debs and the A.R.U. led Darrow to be retained in several other major labor cases during the next twenty years, including the cases of Thomas I. Kidd and the National Association of Wood Workers in 1898, the Anthracite Coal Strike of 1902, Haywood, *et al.* and the Western Federation of Miners in 1905, and the McNamara brothers in 1910. Darrow's career as a labor attorney virtually ended with the defense of the McNamara brothers, when he found himself indicted for conspiracy to bribe a juror in the successful completion of that case. Although he was able to secure a speedy acquittal against the charges, this experience and the advent of the First World War caused Darrow to become active mainly in the practice of criminal law for the remainder of his career.

It is, of course, for this third segment of his legal career that Darrow is best remembered. Although he had previously only dabbled in criminal law on some occasions, this area became his primary concern for the last twenty years of his life. Called in to serve as the trial attorney for over one hundred accused murderers, Darrow was able to save every client from the hangman's noose and nearly one-half of his clients were able to escape imprisonment.[4] Darrow saw only one client fall prey to the executioner, and in this instance he had only taken the case on appeal after the initial judgment had been lost.[5]

In 1924, Darrow was successful in avoiding capital punishment for Richard Loeb and Nathan Leopold, confessed "perfect crime" killers of Bobby Franks. It was within his final argument to the bench during this case that he made an impassioned plea for humanity against the horrors of capital punishment that saved the murderers' lives and won Darrow national recognition. The following year, he served as defense counsel to John T. Scopes in Tennessee's famous "Monkey Trial," and his critical cross-examination of William Jennings Bryan's religious fundamentalism made a mockery of the beliefs of the former three-time Presidential candidate and the rationale for the retention of an anti-evolution statute. In 1926, Darrow successfully defended Dr. Ossian Sweet and ten other Negroes in an emotion-charged case of racial

violence in Detroit; and in 1932 he journeyed to Hawaii to secure freedom for four individuals in another case complicated by violent racial overtones. This final case, the Massie case, marked the end of Darrow's active career as an attorney. He served briefly as the chairman of an investigative commission that reviewed charges against President Franklin Roosevelt's National Recovery Administration, but, for the most part, Darrow's last six years were spent in retirement. Darrow died of pulmonary heart disease in Chicago in 1938 at the age of eighty.[6]

Clarence Darrow—Minority Man

Throughout his career, Clarence Darrow generally occupied the role of spokesman for the interests of various minority groups or points of view. With the exception of his seven years' work as a corporate attorney, Darrow's legal posture was one of defense for the poor and downtrodden of society or for some issue that ran counter to the beliefs of the controlling majority. He was the perennial dissenter, the constant champion of the underdog, and the tireless sarcastic critic of the prevailing social order.[7] It was by this role that he became famous during his lifetime and is best remembered today. Darrow remained undaunted by the fact that his beliefs and positions were often unpopular; Gurko contends that he rather enjoyed this seeming disadvantage:

Like his father, he never minded being one against many or on the losing side; he found any exchange of ideas, against any odds, exhilarating. Even when his listeners were openly hostile to his unconventional ideas, he was not in the least distressed but went right on, never abandoning his good-natured, gently satirical tone and never backing away from his independent views.[8]

Over the years, Darrow championed the causes of academic freedom, religious freedom, and the many components of individual liberty. He lobbied for the rights of organized labor, for the civil rights of Negroes, and for the necessity of social humanitarianism. He opposed violence, ignorance, and all measures that he felt germinated from the seeds of man's narrow inhumanity: prohibition, religious fundamentalism, racial intolerance, economic monopoly, and capital punishment. Darrow's opposition to such ideas and practices was not limited simply to vocal denunciation; he took an active part in some "opposition" organizations, including the cochairmanship (with Arthur Garfield Hays) of the League to Abolish Capital Punishment[9] and the chairmanship of the Debs Amnesty Committee.[10] This consistent defense of the societal underdog led to Darrow's being nicknamed "the big minority man" by his friends.[11]

Clarence Darrow—Public Debater

Besides taking part in numerous court cases over a span of fifty years, Clarence Darrow also was involved in many other areas of public communication. He wrote articles and short stories for national publications, he narrated a film dealing with the evolution of life forms, he presented hundreds of public speeches on a myriad of subjects, and he took part in a large number of public debates and forums.[12] This work centers upon Darrow as a public debater.

During the early decades of the twentieth century, one of the most popular forms of entertainment was the public debate forum, often held under the auspices of the famous Lyceum and Chautauqua banners. Since there was no television, and

since radio and motion pictures were in their infancy, various types of rallies, revivals, and public speaking exhibitions and contests served both to inform and entertain the American public. Besides providing an interesting evening away from home, public debates presented famous speakers who would do battle on the contemporary issues of the time. Because of his interest in so many social issues and his great reputation as an effective courtroom orator, it is not surprising that Clarence Darrow eventually became deeply involved in this public debate activity.

After the completion of the Loeb-Leopold case in 1924, Darrow engaged in a series of debates on national issues for the following five years. These debates were used as a vehicle of pleasure for the famous trial attorney, and he so enjoyed these occasions to debate topical public issues that he often did not accept a fee for his performances and would occasionally even pay his own expenses.[13] In general, Darrow's debate posture was a mirror of that shown in the courtroom. He took issues used in court and attempted to popularize them on a larger level.[14] These debates were considered major public events by the host cities, and Darrow spent most of his spare time engaged in one forensic struggle or another. He planned to curtail even this enjoyable activity upon his initial retirement in 1929, but he was an unfortunate market speculator and the Great Crash brought him back to the public debate forum to earn his livelihood in 1930.[15] This second series of debates, 1930-31, is considered inferior to that of the mid-1920s in that the later debates "were repetitive patchworks of argument drawn from earlier and greater speeches."[16] Regardless of the year, the issues of the debates remained basically the same: individual freedom, Prohibition, capital punishment, and the relationship of man to life and to a supreme being. These were the major concerns of Darrow's public debating from 1924 through 1931.[17]

Despite the fact that Darrow participated in many more public debates and discussions during those seven years than in various courtroom struggles throughout the entirety of his lifetime, Darrow's career as a public advocate has remained largely ignored by students of history and communication. Scholars have tended to emphasize his courtroom advocacy;[18] little has been said concerning Darrow's public advocacy.[19] Since Darrow visualized his public debate career as an extension of his legal career, as an opportunity to popularize and propagandize those issues and causes for which he fought within the courts of law, the examination of Darrow's public advocacy needs to be expanded. Because of their sheer number and philosophical importance in the career of Clarence Darrow, as well as their relationship to the major social events of the times, Darrow's public debates merit greater attention than they have received to the present time. This work is designed to serve as an initiator of such study.

However, since it would be impractical to examine every public debate in which Clarence Darrow took part during the 1920s, this study has been limited to include five debates that are representative of the major issues of concern to Darrow. The five debates to be critically examined are as follows:

1
"Is Capital Punishment a Wise Public Policy?" Darrow vs. Alfred J. Talley in a debate held in New York City on October 26, 1924.

2
"Resolved: That the United States Should Continue the Policy of Prohibition as Defined in the Eighteenth Amendment." Darrow vs. John Haynes Holmes in a debate held in New York City on December 14, 1924.

3
"Is Man A Machine?" Darrow vs. Will Durant in a debate held in New York City on January 8, 1927.

4
"Resolved: That the Prohibition of the Beverage Liquor Traffic is Detrimental to the Public Welfare." Darrow vs. Wayne B. Wheeler in a debate held in New York City on April 23, 1927.

5
"Resolved: That the Immigration Law Discriminating in Favor of the Races of Northern Europe as Opposed to Those of Southern Europe is an Advantage to the United States." Darrow vs. Lothrop Stoddard in a debate held in New York City in early 1929.[20]

The Assessment of Darrow's Debates

Debate may be viewed as an intensive process of communicative competition, wherein two parties do battle over a central unifying issue. The debate process itself is designed to provide a direct clash of two opposing points of view on the same general topic, thereby allowing the viewing/listening audience better to comprehend the major ideas surrounding the topic in question and to make a better, more-informed decision about the topic. For example, one of the most hotly-contested issues of the 1970s is gun control—should the United States undertake a policy of limiting the sale and purchase of handguns by its citizenry? Many advocates of one position or another on the issue have come forth to express their opinions, and these statements can be found in countless magazine articles and congressional speeches. However, the concerned person who wanted to assess the relative merits of the differing points of view would have a difficult time in juxtaposing these points as they are presented in controlled "best foot forward" contexts, and there is no guarantee that those favoring gun control and those opposing gun control will ever deal with the same specific issues. The process of debate, on the other hand, guarantees such a beneficial juxtaposition by bringing together the opposing points of view in one place at the same time. Thus, the strengths and weaknesses of both positions can be more readily seen and, therefore, a better eventual decision concerning the topic can be reached.

It must be remembered, moreover, that no debate takes place in a vacuum. That is, issues do not arise from oblivion, nor do disputes occur within a neutral social environment. On the contrary, issues for and of debate are an integral part of the social setting in which they occur; they both form and are formed by the total surrounding social environment. Because of the interrelationship between debate and its social context, no debate can be considered meaningfully without a careful examination of the events preceding the debate. Again by way of example, the current "debate" over gun control would be meaningless to an outside observer who was not familiar with the problems caused by firearms in this country. The high incidence of murder and assault via handguns provides the reason for debating gun control policies. If our society was not plagued by the problem, there would be no debate on the topic. Each public debate must, therefore, be considered in light of the societal actions and pressures affecting the issues of the debate.

Accordingly, this examination of Clarence Darrow's public debates during the 1920s is presented within the general social context in which they took place. Darrow's rhetorical strategies and lines of argument

within the five selected debates are examined critically in terms of their social setting by a combination of historical, analytical, and evaluative methods. Thus, this present study may be viewed as an intensive piece of rhetorical criticism as defined by Karlyn Campbell:

Rhetorical criticism is the description, analysis, interpretation, and evaluation of persuasive uses of language. These stages in the critical process have three general purposes: (1) to describe discourses accurately and perceptively so that the unique qualities of individual discourses or genres of discourse become clear to the reader; (2) to analyze internal elements and stratagems of discourses, and to describe the relationship between discourses and their cultural contexts and the persuasive forces impinging on them; (3) to make evaluative judgments of discourses based on explicit criteria so that the grounds for evaluation are apparent to the reader. [21]

The first two purposes outlined by Campbell were approached through the extrinsic/intrinsic method advocated by Hillbruner. [22] Two extrinsic factors and two intrinsic factors were considered in this study. The extrinsic factors are the "historical description and analysis of the times" in which the debates took place and the "historical description and analysis of the audience and the occasion" for each debate. Therefore, the debates have been placed in their relationship to the events of the surrounding rhetorical environment, because, as noted by Hillbruner, the "critic's first job . . . is to discover what was happening at the juncture of history in which the speech event took place." [23] In addition, the public stance of Darrow *vis-a-vis* the issues, the reason for each debate, and the components of audience and occasion were investigated to provide as accurate a description of the event as possible. Research histories, newspaper accounts, and the recollection of Darrow's contemporaries have been utilized in this description.

The intrinsic factors studied are the "description and analysis of the speaker's ideas" and the "interpretation and evaluation of the speaker's ideas." Not only are the arguments and positions advanced by Darrow and his opponents described, they are also evaluated. The strategies and arguments employed by Darrow and his opponents were subject to evaluation in relation to what each speaker was trying to do, what he did, and what he should have done. The material for strategy analysis came from the debates themselves and from Darrow's prior activities and rhetorical postures. Studies dealing with Darrow's courtroom strategy were consulted in providing this evaluation.[24]

As a form of rhetorical criticism, this study may, in the terminology of Thonssen and Baird, be classified as judicial criticism:

> . . . it reconstructs a speech situation with fidelity to fact/ it examines this situation carefully in the light of the interaction of speaker, audience, subject, and occasion/ it interprets the data . . . / it formulates a judgment in the light of the philosophical-historical-logical constituents of the inquiry. . . .[25]

Historical and rhetorical considerations have been interwoven in the description, analysis, and evaluation of the material within the Darrow debates.

Darrow's public debates have been examined according to the tenets of forensic confrontation as well as by the techniques of traditional rhetorical criticism. Specifically, the debates have been categorized according to the types of topics or propositions involved in the phrasing of the topic for debate and the presentation of the inherent issues. Thus, the debate with Will Durant centered upon a proposition of fact (a categorical statement that asserts the existence of a specific fact); the debate with Holmes concerned a proposition of policy (a statement dealing with a course of action); and the debates with Talley, Wheeler, and Stoddard involved propositions of value (a statement that asserts an evaluation of an idea, person, or policy).[26] This distinction of proposition types is important in the consideration of the rhetorical strategies and arguments employed by the debaters. The analysis and evaluation of each debate is tempered according to the type of proposition utilized within that debate. In addition, the specific responsibilities of the debaters—as affected by the type of debate proposition in use—are noted for each debate confrontation, and the evaluation of each debate is heavily dependent upon the debaters' upholding of their specific argumentative responsibilities. In short, what each debater *did* versus what each debater *should have done* forms the basis for evaluating the relative strengths and weaknesses of each debate and debater analyzed.

Regardless of the nature of the debate topic, certain operational definitions of various words and terms have been utilized in providing additional material for each debate evaluation. Such definitions are as follows:

Rhetorical Environment . . . The encompassing political, social and economic situation; the importance and significance of topical public issues; and the existing popular attitudes and beliefs on the issues.[27]

Strategy . . . The speaker's overall plan or his approach to the consideration and presentation of ideas in an argumentative framework.[28]

Tactics . . . The speaker's specific approach to implement his overall

6

strategy in dealing with individual matters or subissues. [29]

Prima Facie Case . . . The sum total of the speaker's arguments and lines of reasoning that establish a position worthy of belief and acceptance prior to the presentation of counterarguments. [30]

Factual Evidence . . . The use of statistical materials and/or specific real-life events and actual examples to support one's argumentative position.

Opinionated Evidence . . . The quotation of an expert's opinion to support one's argumentative position.

Verbal Evidence . . . The use of hypothetical examples and analogies to support one's argumentative position.

These definitions are designed to aid the reader in better understanding the evaluation and analysis of each debate presented. As a further aid to comprehension, this examination of Clarence Darrow's public debate career is organized according to the major issues involved, rather than by individual debate. It is hoped that such a framework provides greater cohesion for the entire study.

As an additional aid to clarity, each debate analyzed has been carefully delineated into its major argumentative thrusts as offered by each debater. Thus, a one-page "brief" of the debate's main lines of argument will be found within the writer's analysis of each individual debate, thereby allowing the reader to see quickly the specific positions taken by the debaters within the contest. Darrow's opinions, as well as the opinions of his opponents, stand clear within the context of the debate studied. Careful assessment of the arguments will indicate both the breadth and depth of the speaker's total position.

Following Chapter Seven, there are excerpts from the debates analyzed in the preceding chapters. The attempt has been made to provide the reader with sufficient verbatim excerpts to enhance the "flavor" of the five Darrow debates. The type of language employed, sentence length, the pace of argument, etc. can best be conveyed through a presentation of parts of the debates themselves. Darrow's strengths and weaknesses as a public advocate, which are detailed within the final chapter of this study, become more apparent after an examination of the debate excerpts. His wit, his sarcasm, and his humanitarianism can be found within these selected portions of debates held many decades ago.

Footnotes

1 Irving Stone, *Clarence Darrow for the Defense* (Garden City, 1941), p. 497.

2 Abe C. Ravitz, *Clarence Darrow and the American Literary Tradition* (Cleveland, 1962), pp. 140-141.

3 Stone, p. 5.

4 Alan Hynd, *Defenders of the Damned* (New York, 1960), p. 66.

5 The account of this case, the trial and execution of Patrick Prendergast, is chronicled in Ray Ginger, *Altgeld's America* (New York, 1958), pp. 215-219.

6 The most intensive biographical study of Darrow is Stone's *Clarence Darrow For the Defense*. Another work, based largely on the material collected by Stone and much more readable, is Miriam Gurko, *Clarence Darrow* (New York, 1965). Gurko's study offers nothing really different from that of Stone's work, but it is easier to comprehend although somewhat shallower in scope.

Most general historical volumes contain reference to Darrow and provide some biographical data. The two such reference works suggested by this writer for possible perusal are *The National Cyclopedia of American Biography*, 1939, XXVII, pp. 4-6; and *Dictionary of American Biography*, 1958, XI, Part 2, pp. 141-144.

7 See Martin Maloney, "Clarence Darrow," in *A History and Criticism of American Public Address*, ed. Marie K. Hochmuth (New York, 1955), III, pp. 266; and Horace G. Rahskopf, "The Speaking of Clarence Darrow," in *American Public Address*, ed. Loren Reid (Columbia, 1961), p. 33.

8 Gurko, p. 25.

9 Arthur Garfield Hays, *City Lawyer* (New York, 1942), p. 212; and *New York Times*, February 17, 1929, p. 24.

10 William M. Kunstler, *The Case for Courage* (New York, 1962), p. 234.

11 George G. Whitehead, *Clarence Darrow–The Big Minority Man* (Girard, 1929), p. 5.

12 Darrow's noncourtroom activity is synthesized by Gurko, p. 270.

13 This factor of enjoyment is mentioned often by Whitehead, *op. cit.* Whitehead, director of publicity of the Redpath Lyceum Bureau, served as the manager of Darrow's debates in 1928 and those of 1930 and 1931. See also Gurko, p. 94.

14 Maloney, p. 298.

15 Hynd, p. 87.

16 Maloney, p. 295.

17 Arthur Weinberg, ed., *Attorney For the Damned* (New York, 1957); and Arthur and Lila Weinberg, eds., *Verdicts Out of Court* (Chicago, 1963) provide illustration of the topics covered in the Darrow debates.

18 See, for example, John B. Roberts, "The Speech Philosophy of Clarence Darrow" (Master's Thesis, State University of Iowa, 1941); James M. Starr, "The Methods of Proof Used by Clarence Darrow in the Loeb-Leopold Murder Trial" (Master's Thesis, University of Washington, 1943); Howard L. Shine, "A Critical Analysis of the Persuasive Techniques in the Trial of John T. Scopes" (Master's Thesis, Bowling Green State University, 1958); David H. Grover, "Debaters and Dynamiters: The Rhetoric of the Haywood Trial" (Ph.D. Dissertation, University of Oregon, 1962); John C. Livingston, "Clarence Darrow: Sentimental Rebel" (Ph.D. Dissertation, University of Wisconsin, 1965); Akira Sanbonmatsu, "Adaptation and Debate Strategies in the Speaking of Clarence Darrow and Alexander Rorke in *New York vs. Gitlow*" (Ph.D. Dissertation, The Pennsylvania State University, 1968); Richard A. Meissel, "The Rhetoric of Legal Self-Defense: The Socrates-More-Darrow Analog" (Master's Thesis, Queens College, 1971); Martin Maloney, "The Forensic Speaking of Clarence Darrow," *Speech Monographs*, XIV (1947), pp. 111-126; and James H. Jackson, "Clarence Darrow's Plea in Defense of Himself," *Western Speech*, XX (Fall, 1956), pp. 185-195.

19 The only study of Darrow's public advocacy is a superficial one. See Harry W. Greene, "The Debates and Religious Forums of Clarence Darrow"

(Master's Thesis, Northern Illinois University, 1970).

[20] Many of Clarence Darrow's public debates were transcribed and published by Haldeman-Julius Publications of Girard, Kansas. Information supplied to this writer by the Copyright Office of the Library of Congress indicated that the copyright licenses to the five debates covered within this study had expired.

[21] Karlyn Kohrs Campbell, *Critiques of Contemporary Rhetoric* (Belmont, 1972), p. 12.

[22] Anthony Hillbruner, *Critical Dimensions: The Art of Public Address Criticism* (New York, 1966), pp. 9-12; 32; 82; 96-126.

[23] *Ibid.*, p. 9.

[24] Sanbonmatsu noted that Darrow's correspondence and private papers, material that would be an asset in the consideration of perceived speaker strategy, had disappeared from its supposed locale in the Library of Congress. Therefore, this type of primary material is not available for use in this study. Sanbonmatsu, p. 9.

[25] Lester Thonssen and A. Craig Baird, *Speech Criticism* (New York, 1948), p. 18.

[26] Eugene R. Moulton, *The Dynamics of Debate* (New York, 1966), pp. 58-59; Roy V. Wood, *Strategic Debate* (Skokie, 1968), pp. 10-13; Austin J. Freeley, *Argumentation and Debate*, Third Edition (Belmont, 1971), pp. 41-42; Wayne N. Thompson, *Modern Argumentation and Debate* (New York, 1971), pp. 18-20; Douglas Ehninger and Wayne Brockriede, *Decision By Debate* (New York, 1968), pp. 220-228; and James H. McBurney and Glen E. Mills, *Argumentation and Debate*, Second Edition (New York, 1964), pp. 30-32.

[27] Hillbruner, *op. cit.*, pp. 9-10.

[28] Wood, *op. cit.*, p. 4.

[29] *Ibid.*

[30] Freley, *op. cit.*, p. 35.

Chapter Two

The Rhetorical Environment

Clarence Darrow's initial series of debates, 1924 through 1929, occurred within the context of an interesting era in American history. Like most such eras, the decade of the 1920s has undergone significant reinterpretation in recent years that allows the historical/rhetorical critic greater flexibility in the analysis of the issues of that period. Previously, the generally accepted view of the twenties was that of an era of intellectual retrenchment, a time of frivolous pleasure-seeking and national dissipation. The First World War was seen as an intellectual, social, and moral wedge that created a wide gap between the first and third decades of the twentieth century. Consistent with this view, the progressive period was seen to have been demolished by the ravages of war and by the national frivolity of the twenties. People were not concerned with relevant social issues; instead, they plunged into a universal anti-intellectual abyss and concentrated upon acquiring material possessions and lavishing praise upon national heroes such as Babe Ruth and Charles Lindbergh. Thus, the concept of the "Lost Generation" served to symbolize a void that had been created and would exist until the Great Crash in 1929. Suddenly, America would return to its national senses, a great liberal president would be rushed into office, and a plethora of progressive social and economic legislation would remove the bankrupt stagnation of the "Roaring Twenties."[1]

However, despite the relatively widespread acceptance of this point of view, several recent historians have offered alternative conceptualizations of the 1920s. Roderick Nash has argued that the prevailing interpretation of the twenties is too broad to present a meaningful analysis of the issues and activities involved: "The conception of this time as one of resigned cynicism and happy reveling leaves too much American thought and action unexplained to be satisfactory."[2] On the contrary, in Nash's view, the "prewar ideas and ideals continued into the twenties" with scarcely a hitch and the First World War and its aftermath caused Americans "to give even stronger affirmation to values that had allegedly ended by 1920."[3] Thus, this view denies the concept of the "Lost Generation" and insists that the American people were directly interested and involved in the major social issues of the 1920s.

In a similar vein, Paul W. Glad has taken exception to the concept that the Progressive Period was ended by American involvement in the First World War. While Glad has admitted that progressiveness in the 1920s lacked the necessary unity and cohesion to pull together into an effective political action group, he has contended that

Progressive sentiment had by no means disappeared by the decade of the 1920s . . .; progressivism had disintegrated as a movement or series of movements. It had not disappeared, however, for it had passed back into the hands of individual reformers.[4]

Glad's analysis has been supported by Clarke A. Chambers, who has also contended that progressive reform was active during the 1920s:

The passing of time would indicate that new lines of action were being tried out in the confused twenties. Not all of them would prove fruitful of ultimate success; but there was a larger validity and viability to the reform impulse in the Golden Years than most participants then realized and than most critics and scholars have since acknowledged.[5]

In support of this position, Chambers has reviewed the activities of several private social reform organizations that were active during the 1920s—the National Consumers' League, the National Child Labor Committeee, the Women's Trade Union League, and the American Association for Labor Legislation—and he has concluded that these organizations allowed the social reform movement to grow, solidify, and organize, thereby paving the way for the reforms of the New Deal. Such reforms of the 1930s were indebted to the reform leaders of the twenties who "kept alive the tradition of humane liberalism in the years of normalcy."

Thus, the historical/rhetorical critic can perceive two divergent views of the 1920s. One holds that this was an era of national dissipation wherein the desire for Harding's "normalcy" caused a societal breakdown in intellectual, social, and moral progress. The period is seen as one of retrenchment between the progressive and New Deal reforms of the early 1900s. The other view holds that although there was a desire for normalcy, the 1920s did display many manifestations of the reform elements from prewar years. It is contended that the prior view of a period of national dissipation overlooks many of the ideals and activities that were an integral part of the framework of the 1920s.

The 1920s—Era of Societal Dissonance

Regardless of the overall view of the decade that the particular analyst happens to hold, it cannot be denied that many significant social questions and problems were prevalent during the 1920s. However, because the many specific issues were so varied and covered a wide scope of thought and action, it is difficult to understand the many complexities involved. Nonetheless, the application of homeostasis theory to the 1920s will reveal that this was an era of massive societal dissonance.

Homeostasis theory is based upon the concept that people, both individually and collectively, seek to maintain a balance between their intellectual, social, moral, and ethical views and that which is perceived as occurring within the surrounding environment. This desire for cognitive balance has been summed up by Festinger: ". . . the human organism tries to establish internal harmony, consistency, or congruity among his opinions, attitudes, knowledge, and values."[6] Thus, if the individual is confronted with a situation, concept, or action that fails to balance with his predispositions, then an imbalance is created within the individual that requires corrective action: "The existence of dissonance, being psychologically uncomfortable, will motivate the person to try to reduce the dissonance and achieve consonance."[7]

Did a dissonant condition exist during the 1920s? Nash has suggested that it did:

The generation that entered the twenties had participated in events both dramatic and commonplace, which combined to alter the American scene at an accelerating and bewildering pace . . . . Bewilderment and insecurity are not

12

acceptable conditions for most persons . . . . Americans from 1917 to 1930 constituted a nervous generation, groping for what certainty they could find. [8]

Because of the changes that marked the decade of the 1920s, the American people found themselves confronted with a massive condition of dissonance. "Normalcy" was nothing more than an intense national desire to return to the verities and certainties of the past. Nash's "nervous generation" is but another term for "national societal dissonance."

However, it is not sufficient merely to recognize that a dissonant condition existed during the 1920s nor to suggest the causes of the condition. Festinger has noted that individuals do not accept dissonant conditions as part of their permanent social structure; when such conditions arise, they attempt to "try to reduce the dissonance and achieve consonance." It is this attempt at dissonance-reduction that best characterizes the rhetorical environment of the 1920s, and it is with the particular strains and stresses operating within that society that the remainder of this chapter is concerned.

Reaction to the First World War

On April 2, 1917, Woodrow Wilson faced a joint session of Congress and attempted to set the philosophical rationale for American involvement in the First World War:

The world must be made safe for democracy. Its peace must be planted upon the tested foundations of political liberty. We have no selfish ends to serve. We desire no conquest, no dominion. We seek no indemnities for ourselves, no material compensation for the sacrifices we shall freely make. We are but one of

the champions of the rights of mankind . . . we shall fight for the things which we have always carried nearest our hearts–for democracy, for the right of those who submit to authority to have a voice in their own governments . . . . [9]

Thus, according to Wilson, the United States entered the war with the highest of ideals and motives in its call to arms. There was no desire to expand the national power nor to increase the nation's territorial size. Instead, American involvement was based upon the desire to make the world "safe for democracy." The American people adopted the rationale advocated by President Wilson:

The American nation entered World War I in the same exuberant spirit with which during the Progessive Era it had crusaded for the reconstruction of society at home . . . . If the premises upon which the Wilsonian policy rested could be implemented, progress toward the winning of that ancient dream of brotherhood, justice, and peace would be assured. [10]

However, with the cessation of hostilities in 1918, it soon became apparent that the ideal of international brotherhood and justice was to be a dream unfulfilled. The squabbling at the peace conference at Versailles indicated that the European allies were more concerned with territorial and economic aggrandizement than with the achievement of lofty democratic ideals. The concern arose that the United States had been tricked into entering the war unwittingly to aid the national designs of England, France, and Italy. In short, a negative reaction against the war set in, and the national compulsion for idealism, as best exemplified by President Wilson, quickly waned. [11]

With the disillusionment concerning

13

American involvement in international affairs, there was a concomitant decline in the viability of similar idealistic activities on the domestic level. Optimism tended to be dimmed by the realities of postwar America. It was apparent that no general moral and ethical uplift had been generated by wartime activity; the American consumer was faced with an inflation in market prices, and the American farmer saw the bottom drop out of his war-inflated economy.[12] National idealism declined as America entered the postwar world.

The result of this decline in national optimism was the concomitant decline in both the existence and the effectiveness of national progressive reform sentiment. This is not to say that the progressive spirit was dead, but progressivism was definitely hampered by the anti-idealism fostered by the disillusionment with the war. Progressives were no longer confident that their desired reforms could produce needed changes in society and they lacked the ability to transform their ideals into an effective political force.[13] Limited by the social pessimism of the early 1920s, the progressive movement operated on a more individualistic basis during this decade than it had during prewar years:

Turned back again and again, they began to pioneer new methods and posit new goals. Out of defeat was born the desire to seek out new paths of reform, new roads to Zion. Out of frustration was born social reconstruction, devices that anticipated much of the central program of the New Deal. The high enthusiasm with which some had predicted immediate reconstruction of American society at the end of the war proved not justified, but neither were the years of the twenties the wasteland for reform that they have frequently seemed. [14]

Thus, the progressive reform movement was modified by the war-related social pessimism that marked the early 1920s. From this conflict emerged many of the salient social issues that were manifested in Clarence Darrow's public debates: the feasibility of uplifting man's humanity toward his fellow man, the continued need for humane reforms, and the practicality of various social reform programs.

Fear of Internal Revolution

It has been often noted in panegyrical Independence Day rhetoric that one of the most outstanding attributes of American society and government is the tolerance shown toward attitudes and opinions that run contrary to the norm. American tolerance of unpopular beliefs has been touted as a benchmark of the American Republic, perhaps unjustifiably. Certainly, in the decade following the First World War, the tolerance of and the expression of minority views provided a second area of societal dissonance:

Frightened men unwilling to confront the problems of the new America coming into being preferred to blame the difficulties about them on the heretics and the strangers. Such fears ultimately made the alien and the radical scapegoats for the country's ills . . . [yet] many Americans resisted the dominant trend and maintained a view of liberty broad enough to leave dissent unfettered and to protect the rights of aliens. The interplay of the two sets of forces provides the drama [of the account of this time period]. [15]

Similar to the growth of anti-idealism and social negativism, the growth of intolerance toward unpopular views during the 1920s stemmed, in large part, from the First World War. While it is certainly true that the anti-radicalism that marked the 1920s

14

had its roots in prewar ideologies and activities, the nature of the war on the domestic front was responsible for molding the intolerance of the 1920s.[16]

To prosecute the war effort successfully, the Wilson administration had deluged the country with a massive propaganda campaign to secure total compliance with the mobilization program. This campaign fell under the direction of George Creel's Committee on Public Information:

. . . it had preached patriotism to the American public by means of the written word, spoken word, motion picture, signboard, and poster, and had so directed its propaganda that 'every printed bullet might reach its mark.' The public press had followed in the pattern set by the committee and the net result had been an indoctrination of hate, prejudice, and 100 percent Americanism on a colossal scale . . . . Under such circumstances the free play of opinion and the opportunity for independent action had practically ceased to exist.[17]

Largely through the efforts of Creel's committee, American opinion had been mobilized to provide complete support for the war effort against the uncivilized "Huns" of the Central Powers.

However, the creation of intolerance for anything that was not "100 percent Americanism" did not abate with the cessation of hostilities in 1918. As Allen has noted, this intolerant hysteria was manifested against any thought or action believed to be of un-American origin or import:

The emotions of group loyalty and of hatred expanded during wartime and then suddenly denied their intended expression, found a perverted release in the persecution not only of supposed radicals, but also of other elements which to the dominant American group—the
white Protestants—seemed alien or 'un-American.'[18]

Intolerance, then, was transferred from the war effort to an intolerance toward unpopular beliefs during the 1920s.

This hysteria was given impetus by the events immediately following the First World War. The economic inflation that beset the United States caused many laborers to strike for increased wages to deal with inflationary pressures. Some violence occurred, several people were killed, and the loyalty of the labor movement was gravely questioned. In addition, there were undoubtedly some *bona fide* radicals who desired to overthrow the government of the United States and to form a government modeled upon that of Soviet Russia. Occasional bombings and industrial sabotage only served to provide demonstrable proof that the United States was in danger of an immense radical revolt, thereby justifying the repression of unpopular thought and action.[19] The purported threat to the country was particularly advocated by men (such as Attorney General A. Mitchell Palmer) who desired to benefit from the existence of this threat:

. . . The Red Scare of the 1920s introduced a new permanent dimension of intolerance. This was the aspiring, self-seeking individual or special-interest group which sought to exploit the hysteria and intolerance of the moment for personal advantage . . . ; the ability to project themselves into the role of master defender of the endangered order could mean nomination to high office . . . .[20]

However, although it might be true that the great majority of Americans participated in this wave of intolerance,[21] there still existed those who opposed the repression of the alien and radical components of the national community, preferring instead to uphold the traditional dedication to free expression of ideas, no matter how unpopular they might be. The existence of both groups created the second area of societal dissonance, wherein two conflicting forces claimed the same goal: the maintenance of the spirit of America. This societal conflict was manifested in the immigration restrictions of the 1920s and the debates over how far free expression should be allowed to extend. Clarence Darrow became embroiled in this controversy in both the courts of law, such as in *Gitlow vs. New York*, and in debates on the public platform.

Reaction to Urbanization and Industrialization

The early decades of the twentieth century in the United States marked the transformation of a rural country into a highly urbanized and industrialized nation. Influenced by the needs of increased technology, the pressures for wartime industrial production, and the increased use of mechanization in farming, many ruralites left the farming areas to seek employment in large urban centers. Immigrants entering the country tended to migrate to the large cities to establish ethnic ghettos of familiarity and cooperation. Then, with the aftermath of the First World War and the poor economic conditions in America's farm belt and throughout Europe, emigration to the urban areas increased dramatically.[22] While many Americans saw this transformation as generally necessary and beneficial, the actual shift itself created another factor of societal dissonance:

Many Americans felt uneasy as they experienced the transforming effects of population growth, urbanization, and economic change. On the one hand, these

developments were welcome as steps in the direction of progress. Yet they also raised vague fears about the passing of frontier conditions, the loss of national vigor, and the eclipse of the individual in a mass society.[23]

The dissonance created by this shift was manifested in a split between members of socioeconomic classes and between the urban-rural sections of the nation. Although it cannot be said that an intellectual or philosophical "civil war" was created, it can be maintained that the dissonance caused a definite splintering of the universal harmony that had marked the nation's efforts during the First World War. Prohibition, religious fundamentalism, and restrictions on the flow of immigration were affected by the split.

The rural distaste for the dramatic increase in urbanization can be traced to two sources. First, as the number of people remaining on the land rapidly declined, those who stayed felt an increasing economic pinch. With mass urbanization, there was a concomitant demand for increased governmental services, and, because of the nature of state revenue procurement, the cost of these urban-oriented services fell upon the farmer:

The costs of government were being multiplied at the local level by new kinds of schools with more teachers receiving better pay, and at the state level by increased services, larger bureaucracies, and higher salaries. Farmers were the primary source of government income, but the number of farmers was dwindling. As a result, the per capita tax load for those who remained was even higher than it would have been with a stable farm population.[24]

Thus, the farmer looked upon the urban areas with a jaundiced eye, claiming that it was his money that allowed the cities to grow while he received nothing in return. Rural distaste for urbanization had, to some extent, an economic base.

Second, there was an urban-rural split because of a fundamental difference in lifestyles and ways of viewing the proper activities in implementing these lifestyles. As Kirschner has noted:

These collisions involved the kinds of differences that grow from attitudes, customs, traditions, and values. In other words, they involved opposite ways of looking at life rather than opposite ways of making a living. [25]

Specifically, the farm belt seriously questioned the virility and morality of the mode of life within the cities. Agrarian areas viewed themselves as the last bastions of rugged Americanism:

Farmers were the only true democrats. They were the best representatives of the American tradition. The cities held the idle rich and the owners of mortgages and the dregs of Europe. [26]

In response to these rural objections, it became somewhat fashionable within urban centers to poke fun at the rural existence. Whereas it had been an American tradition to eulogize the farmer and the agrarian way of life, the 1920s witnessed the increased popularity of writers such as H. L. Mencken, Edgar Lee Masters, Sinclair Lewis, and F. Scott Fitzgerald, who

. . . represented a trend that was making it fashionable either to mount a literary assault on farm and village, or to praise the virtues of city life. The message of the new literature was perceived—sometimes vaguely, sometimes quite directly—and resented in the countryside. [27]

Although Clarence Darrow did not debate the supposed advantages of city living compared to living on the farm, or *vice versa*, he did become embroiled in those issues that represented the urban-rural split: religious fundamentalism, Prohibition, and immigration restrictions.

Reaction to Variation in the Social Order

Closely related to the aforementioned social issue, the fourth factor of societal dissonance springs from the massive variation that marked the social order during the 1920s. On the one hand, rural America retained a heavy nineteenth century flavor; on the other, urban America demonstrated a new lifestyle and a new type of morality. The conflict of these two competing elements created a societal imbalance that led to reactions and counterreactions throughout the decade. The problem was not merely that rural superiority was giving away to the growth of the urban centers; the problem stemmed from a perceived shift and dichotomy of value patterns. [28]

It has been previously noted that ruralites distrusted those living in the city and tended to vilify the concept of city living itself. This distrust, moreover, was deeper than a superficial objection to a foreign way of life; this distrust was a manifestation of a perceived moral and ethical dichotomy that existed between the city and the country. To the farmer, the city was a den of indecency and depravity:

Increasingly, he [the farmer] removed the capitalist from his economic context and abstracted him to a kind of generalized symbol of indecency . . . . As farmers saw it, the capitalist was unable to create a meaningful existence in the city, and so he and his family dulled their senses in a kind of Roman voluptuousness that was utterly depraved. [29]

17

To the ruralite, the city became the symbol of free-wheeling immorality, godlessness, and bomb-throwing radicalism. It was the city that housed the capitalist who foreclosed the farmer's mortgage, it was the city that sheltered the Jews, the Catholics, and the other races and ethnic groups that were attempting to "de-Americanize" America. The ruralite desperately desired to return to the stricter moral order of the simpler nation that existed in the past.[30] Nothing "seemed more dangerous to the fundamental beliefs" of the ruralite than the existence of the urban millions.[31]

This perceived dichotomy had an important impact upon the life and activities of Clarence Darrow. Either directly or indirectly, it caused his involvement in several major court cases (Gitlow, Scopes, and Sweet) and his involvement in public debate upon the subissues that stemmed from this dichotomy. Although a ruralite by birth and upbringing, Darrow became identified with the urban interests of his adopted home of Chicago. It would be his lot to serve as the *de facto* spokesman of the urban interests when the rural-urban dichotomy touched his legal and nonlegal activities.

Societal Dissonance—Catalyst for Social Confrontation

The existence of a dissonant condition within an individual or group of individuals produces a feeling of psychological imbalance and discomfort. Therefore, a course of action is followed to relieve the dissonant condition. The issues about which Clarence Darrow assumed a public posture during the 1920s stemmed from efforts to reduce a dissonant condition and the reactions to this attempt at such a reduction.

The battle over Prohibition stemmed, in part, from the urban-rural split that deepened during the 1920s.[32] The decrease in the level of tolerance for minority opinions and the harsh restrictions placed upon immigration, as well as the rebirth of the Ku Klux Klan, were largely based upon vague fears generated by the Bolshevik Revolution and the urban-rural mutual distrust.[33] The renewed battle both for and against strict religious fundamentalism was part of a nation's attempt to secure "normalcy" to reduce dissonance. Capital punishment, although not as directly affected as a philosophy by the nature of the time, became an important issue for proposed social action during the 1920s. Its detractors claimed that it was cruel and inhumane; its supporters claimed that it was the last mode of retaliation against the subversive and criminal element that was about to bring America to its knees.

Clarence Darrow's public debates occurred within an interesting and critical period in American history. The events and the issues of the times were not discrete, separate entities; all were deeply interwoven in the cloth of societal dissonance. Festinger has noted that

. . . the presence of pressures to reduce dissonance, or even activity directed toward such reduction, does not guarantee that the dissonance will be reduced . . . it is quite conceivable that in the process of trying to reduce dissonance, it might even be increased.[34]

The issues that stemmed from this attempted dissonance reduction were the major social issues of the 1920s and they were the main components of Darrow's public speaking activities.

Footnotes

[1] This view of the 1920s is represented by Mark Sullivan, *Our Times: The United States, 1900-1925* (New York, 1935), and by Dumas Malone and Basil Rauch, *War and Troubled Peace, 1917-1939* (New York, 1960). It is fairly safe to assert that the majority of general surveys continue to reflect the "Lost Generation" concept of the 1920s.

[2] Roderick Nash, *The Nervous Generation, American Thought, 1917-1930* (Chicago, 1970), p. 2.

[3] *Ibid.*, p. 3.

[4] Paul W. Glad, "Progressives and the Business Culture of the 1920s," *The Journal of American History*, LIII (June, 1966), 81 and 89.

[5] Clarke A. Chambers, *Seedtime of Reform–American Social Service and Social Action, 1918-1933* (Minneapolis, 1963), p. xi.

[6] Leon Festinger, *A Theory of Cognitive Dissonance* (New York, 1957), p. 260.

[7] *Ibid.*, p. 3.

[8] Nash, pp. v and 2.

[9] T. Woodrow Wilson, "War Messages," in *Selected American Speeches on Basic Issues*, edited by Carl G. Brandt and Edward M. Shafter, Jr. (Boston, 1960), pp. 308 and 310.

[10] Chambers, p. 3.

[11] See Nash, p. 40; and Frederick Lewis Allen, *Only Yesterday* (New York, 1931), pp. 16-20.

[12] Don S. Kirschner, *City and Country–Rural Responses to Urbanization in the 1920s* (Westport, 1970), pp. 1-2.

[13] Glad, pp. 75 and 81.

[14] Chambers, p. 26.

[15] William Preston, Jr., *Aliens and Dissenters–Federal Suppression of Radicals, 1903-1933* (Cambridge, 1963), p. viii.

[16] *Ibid.*, pp. 240-241.

[17] Robert K. Murray, *Red Scare: A Study of National Hysteria, 1919-1920* (New York, 1955), pp. 12-13. The particular workings of the Committee on Public Information has been chronicled in George Creel, *How We Advertised America* (New York, 1920).

[18] Allen, p. 44.

[19] Murray's work provides an excellent description and analysis of the presumed radical threat to the United States during the early 1920s. See, especially, pp. 33-56.

[20] Paul L. Murphy, "Sources and Nature of Intolerance in the 1920s," *The Journal of American History*, LI (June, 1964), p. 66.

[21] *Ibid.*, p. 61.

[22] Kirschner, p. 13.

[23] Nash, p. 126.

[24] Kirschner, p. 6.

[25] *Ibid.*, p. 76.

[26] Andrew Sinclair, *Prohibition: The Era of Excess* (Boston, 1962), p. 13.

[27] Kirschner, pp. 16-17.

[28] Murphy, p. 68.

[29] Kirschner, pp. 23-25.

[30] Nash, p. 145.

[31] Sinclair, p. 64.

[32] See Sinclair, pp. 5-19; Kirschner, pp. 130-131; Nash, p. 145.

[33] See Nash, pp. 143-144; Murphy, p. 75.

[34] Festinger, p. 23.

Chapter Three

Capital Punishment

During its 1972 summer term, the United States Supreme Court created a national furor by declaring that, because of its inequitable application and use throughout the states, capital punishment was an unconstitutional criminal penalty.[1] Opponents of the death penalty hailed the decision as one that would ultimately advance the cause of humanity in the prevention of crime and the rehabilitation of convicted felons. Proponents of the death penalty expressed fears that the Supreme Court decision would herald a massive wave of lawlessness, reasoning that it was only the fear of death that would effectively prevent the commission of criminal acts. Since that decision, several states have moved to reinstitute the use of capital punishment for the commission of specified crimes, thereby meeting the criterion of "uniform application" as decreed by the Supreme Court.

The contemporary debate surrounding the practicality, viability, and effectiveness of capital punishment is not unique to modern history. The advantages and disadvantages of capital punishment have been debated since Biblical times, and the major arguments for either position have not been altered significantly by the passage of time.[2] Those who have advocated the use of capital punishment have tended to argue that it is beneficial for its deterrent effect upon the commission of other crimes. In short, they have reasoned, if an individual realized that he may lose his life if he perpetrates a certain crime, then it is highly unlikely that the individual will commit that crime. In addition, it is often contended that it is only capital punishment that gives full, driving force to the nation's laws. Without capital punishment, there would be no penalty that would effectively check the ever-present criminal menace.

Those who have advocated the abolition of capital punishment have generally combined a philosophical and pragmatic approach in their advocacy. The opponents of the death penalty have argued that man does not have the moral right to take the life of another and that such "legalized murder" has a deleterious effect upon the state and its citizenry, a point exemplified by Beccaria in the eighteenth century:

The punishment of death is pernicious to society, from the example of barbarity it affords. If the passions, or the necessity of war, have taught men to shed the blood of their fellow-creatures, the laws, which are intended to moderate the ferocity of mankind, should not increase it by examples of barbarity, the more horrible as this punishment is usually attended with formal pageantry. Is it not absurd, that the laws, which detest and punish homicide, should, in order to prevent murder, publicly commit murder themselves?[3]

Besides having this adverse effect, it has also been argued that there is no correlation between capital punishment and the deterrence of crime. Therefore, because its disadvantages outweigh any purported advantages, capital punishment should not be utilized.

In the United States, the first attempt to limit the use of capital punishment occurred in 1794 in the state of Pennsylvania; Michigan became the first state to abolish its use, except in cases of treason, in 1847. By the time of the Darrow-Talley debate on capital punishment in 1924, some six states had abandoned its use.[4]

Darrow's Posture on Capital Punishment

While Clarence Darrow was practicing law in various small towns throughout northeastern Ohio, he often occupied his spare moments by reading books and magazine articles that dealt with the practice of law and with the punishments inflicted under the law. In 1884, he came across a recently published work by Judge John Peter Altgeld of Chicago, entitled *Our Penal Machinery and Its Victims,* and the influence of this work and its author was to leave a mark upon Darrow for the remainder of his life.[5] When Darrow migrated to Chicago, the first person he ventured to meet was John P. Altgeld.

To understand Altgeld's influence upon Darrow, one need only look at portions of the 1884 manuscript and juxtapose them to Darrow's later pronouncements about the causes and prevention of crime. For example, Darrow often claimed that capital punishment was ineffective in the prevention of crime, that it was not a deterrent force:

The truth is, that what is called crime is not prevented by fear of punishment. It has never been influenced that way. This is due to causes that are not always clear and distinct and readily understood. No amount of cruelty and threatening can affect the cause.[6]

Altgeld had presented the same concept years before, and the younger attorney apparently accepted the older man's contention:

In the entire history of the human race there is not a single instance in which

cruelty effected a genuine reformation. It can crush, but it cannot improve. It can restrain, but as soon as the restraint is removed the subject is worse than before. The human mind is so constituted that it must be led toward the good, and can be driven in only one direction, and that is toward ruin.[7]

Another example of the Altgeld influence upon Darrow is provided by an examination of the oft-used Darrow contention that man was not wholly responsible for his criminal actions. Prominent New York attorney Arthur Garfield Hays summed up Darrow's philosophy on this point of nonculpability:

Darrow always regarded his clients as victims of misfortune . . . . Consistent with his ingrained philosophy he showed that the individual is moved by forces beyond his control and that the legal theory of individual responsibility was wholly contrary to scientific facts.[8]

Darrow argued that man was not responsible for his actions; instead, man was but a product of heredity and environment, and there was no rationale for punishing man for the imperfections of all men:

The history of the past is a record of man's cruel inhumanity to man–of one imperfect vessel accusing and shattering another for the faults of both . . . . [The world] has penned and maimed, tortured and killed, because the potter's work was imperfect and the clay was weak . . . . Every jail, every scaffold, every victim, is a monument to its cruelty and blind unreasoning wrath . . . . There might be some excuse if man could turn from the frail, cracked vessels, and bring to trial the great potter for the imperfect work of his hand.[9]

The similarity of Darrow's position to that of Altgeld is demonstrated by turning to the 1884 manuscript:

They [criminals] are tools, not

masters–mere instruments, not
principals, and, so far as it concerns
moral responsibility, might as well be
inanimate and unconscious. Yet we treat
them as if they were masters. [10]

Thus, it is apparent that Altgeld had
an influence upon Darrow's concept
of the causality of crime and upon the
infeasibility of the law's placing
specific blame upon the individual
for his actions. Both points were to
prove to be significant in the
Darrow-Talley clash, a debate that
occurred some forty years after
Altgeld's work was published.

Besides writing and speaking against
the death penalty and calling for
various penal reforms, John Peter
Altgeld also attempted to utilize the
legislative process to implement his
desired modifications in the criminal
justice system. In 1895, he vainly
attempted to persuade the Illinois
Legislature to reconsider the viability
of capital punishment:

I respectfully submit for your
consideration the question as to whether
the death penalty does any substantial
good, whether we are any better off than
they are in those States where they long
ago abolished it, whether it is not
barbarous and degrading in its effects,
and whether it would not be better to have
a more rational system of managing our
prisons, and then abolish capital
punishment entirely. [11]

Although Governor Altgeld's plea
accomplished no change in Illinois'
criminal justice system, it inspired
Darrow to attempt similar legislative
persuasion. Elected to the Illinois
House of Representatives in 1902,
Darrow spent most of his term in the
futile attempt to eliminate the use
of the death penalty. It was the only
elective office that he ever held, and
it was the only cause for which he so
desperately worked and so miserably
failed. [12] Because of this two-year
failure, Darrow refused to stand for

re-election, preferring to argue for
the abolition of capital punishment in
various courts of law and in the
public forum. Although he became a
member and chairman of the League
to Abolish Capital Punishment in
1929, Darrow's major anti-death
penalty advocacy was that of an
individual citizen pleading for
humanity and kindness in the system
of law. [13]

Whether Darrow's opposition to
capital punishment stemmed from
his own morbid fear of death, from
an unrecorded childhood experience,
or from a humanistic concern for the
lives of all men is relatively
unimportant for this study. What is
important, however, is that this
opposition to capital punishment was
a central mainstay of Darrow's life
philosophy throughout his legal
career. Historian Ray Ginger has
correctly concluded that Darrow's
philosophical tenets tended to shift
and become contradictory with the
passage of time. [14] Such was not the
case with his attitudes toward capital
punishment. From as early as 1884
until his death in 1938, Clarence
Darrow was an impassioned,
outspoken critic of the death penalty,
and the year 1924 provided two
public forums in which to espouse
his cause for the abolition of capital
punishment.

The Loeb-Leopold Trial

In May of 1924, there occurred one of
the most celebrated murder cases in
the history of American
jurisprudence: the murder of Robert
Franks and the subsequent
prosecution of the alleged murderers,
Richard Loeb and Nathan Leopold.
The fact of the murder was not the
reason for its notoriety; the cause of
the murder and the background of its
perpetrators made it a sensational
public concern.

It was not a crime of vengeance, it was not a crime to secure material possessions, and it was not a crime of passion. The killing of Bobby Franks was a killing for the mere thrill of killing, the culmination of a desire to commit a perfect crime. Thus, unlike other murders, the victim was not the primary concern in the murder plan; the plan itself was of utmost concern to Loeb and Leopold. Bobby Franks just happened to be the unfortunate third party whose death had to occur to consummate the murder scheme.

Not only was the wantonness of the killing a reason for the case's notoriety, the background of the murderers was also significant in creating a national sensation. Both Loeb and Leopold came from extremely wealthy families, both had been given almost every possible advantage that one might enjoy, and both boys were of superior intellect and academic achievement. Thus, the usual factors that underlie the reason for murder were not present in the killing of Bobby Franks. Instead, all that was present was the death of a fourteen-year-old boy at the hands of two would-be "perfect" criminals.

The outcry of public indignation against the commission of such a crime was overwhelming. The citizenry of Chicago, as well as most of the country, cried for vengeance, demanding that the murderers be quickly brought to trial, adjudged guilty, and then hanged as quickly as possible. The mass media served to stir the flames of public outrage with detailed exposition of the specifics of the crime and the needless loss of a young boy whose future knew no bounds. Into this morass of wanton premeditated murder and public outcry for vengeance stepped Clarence Darrow in mid-1924.

Darrow's decision to join the defense of Loeb and Leopold engendered a wave of unfavorable criticism. People proclaimed that the wealth of the defendants' families was being used to circumvent justice by hiring this skillful judicial advocate. Darrow was castigated as unprincipled, as a man more concerned with the lining of his wallet than with the assurance that justice would be satisfied.

Darrow realized before accepting the invitation to take part in the defense of Loeb and Leopold that his decision would be impugned as financial in nature. Nonetheless, he believed that the boys deserved the best defense possible in very negative circumstances and felt that the purpose of such defense was only to prevent the execution of Loeb and Leopold, not to attempt to set them free from custody.[15] Because the two boys, after intense questioning by the police, had admitted killing Franks, Darrow chose to argue the case without a jury to minimize the amount of prejudicial opinion in the final decision by the court. Instead, the entirety of the case was argued before Judge John R. Caverly, and it was upon this man that the fate of the confessed murderers fell.[16]

Without attempting to describe the intricacies of the various forensic strategies employed by Darrow in defending Loeb and Leopold, it is significant to note the major line of argumentation utilized in that defense. Basically, Darrow's plea was composed of two arguments: first, that Loeb and Leopold were too young to be put to death, and, second, that capital punishment was inhuman and counterproductive. These major arguments were presented and developed via the following substructure:

I. Capital Punishment is Inhuman
    A. Capital punishment is a regression to the past
    B. Enlightened, civilized thought rejects capital punishment
    C. Capital punishment is no better than murder itself

II. Capital Punishment is
Counterproductive
  A. The motivations behind crime
     are not eradicated
  B. The murder victim is not
     benefited
  C. Capital punishment does not
     assure justice nor deter crime
III. Capital Punishment is
Unprecedented in this Case
  A. Minors have not received the
     death penalty
  B. The judge must decide upon
     the question of death

By combining an indictment of capital punishment with a plea for mercy due to the youth of the defendants, Darrow was able to weave a powerful plea in which the burden was thrust totally upon the shoulders of Judge Caverly. Darrow hoped that, by placing the sole responsibility for the exercise of the death penalty upon Caverly, Loeb and Leopold might receive a sentence of life imprisonment.

The final summation by Darrow lasted nearly twelve hours and had a visible effect upon Judge Caverly. After nearly three weeks of study, Caverly announced that Loeb and Leopold were to be sentenced to consecutive terms of ninety-nine years plus life imprisonment. Although there is no precise method of determining the effect of Darrow's arguments upon the decision, it plainly encompassed the burden Darrow sought to crystallize:

. . . he [Judge Caverly] was moved to that alternative [imprisonment, not death] by a consideration of the age of the defendants . . . and his unwillingness to impose a sentence of death on persons not of full age. Such a sentence, he concluded, was in accordance with the progress of the criminal law all over the world and all of the dictates of an enlightened humanity.[17]

Clarence Darrow's advocacy had served to spare the lives of Richard Loeb and Nathan Leopold, and the decision by Judge Caverly was viewed similarly to the more recent view of the Supreme Court decision of June 1972. It touched off waves of relief and of indignation that varied according to one's own predisposition toward the issue of capital punishment. The *New York Times* carried two pages of comment upon the decision and concluded in its own editorial that "the deterrent effect on the criminally disposed may not be what hanging would have been."[18] The question of the fate of Loeb and Leopold quickly became secondary to the overall question of the viability and utility of capital punishment itself. A great public debate ensued, and Clarence Darrow found a second major forum for his anti-capital punishment crusade.

The Darrow-Talley Debate

Eleven days after the announcement of the decision in the Loeb-Leopold case, Clarence Darrow was in New York City to speak at a dedication ceremony of that city's Neuropathic Hospital. The directors of that institution had decided to embark upon a prolonged study of the cognitive causes of criminal activity and had asked Darrow to speak upon the need for such study. Darrow, the leading exponent of the theory that held that criminal actions were based on individual mental defects, accepted the invitation and, during the course of the ceremony, indicted the contemporary mode of the study and punishment of crime:

The fact is, that were it not so sad, it would be laughable to think that we are spending millions annually on the prosecution of crime while practically nothing is being done to prevent it.

In considering crime, its cause and effect, the world must first be made to understand that so long as all human conduct has a cause, it becomes the duty of civilization to learn that cause instead of devoting itself blindly to a study and punishment of the effects of evil human conduct. [19]

The following day, Judge Alfred J. Talley of New York City's Court of General Sessions challenged Darrow's view of crime and the proper treatment of criminals. In a statement released to the New York press, Talley declared that people like Darrow wanted to "coddle" criminals and that such attitudes toward crime and its perpetrators had to be ended. As to the specific contention that criminals were often the "effects" of latent mental and societal "causes," Talley responded:

It is not the criminals, actual or potential, that need a neuropathic hospital. It is the people who slobber over them in an effort to find excuses for their crimes.

Those who worry about the mentality of criminals should know that a recent survey of the mentality of prisoners in Joliet Prison by neurologists and psychologists disclosed that the mental status of about 2,000 prisoners was exactly on a par with the mental equipment of our American Expeditionary Army. In other words, about the average.

There are lots of sick people who concern themselves with crime, but the criminals are not numbered among them. [20]

Because of Judge Talley's outspoken criticism of Darrow's concepts of the causes of crime and because the jurist had scathingly indicted the decision in the Loeb-Leopold case, the directors of the League for Public Discussion decided that a debate between Darrow and Talley on some aspect of criminology would be of public interest. Since the Loeb-Leopold case was still drawing attention and comment, it was finally decided that the topic of debate would center upon the viability of the death penalty in the American criminal justice system. [21]

Thus, on mid-Sunday afternoon, October 26, 1924, Clarence Darrow and Alfred J. Talley squared off in a two-hour debate before some three thousand people at the Manhattan Opera House. [22] The League for Public Discussion had advertised the debate as a monumental clash between two of the leading opponents in the national debate on the utilization of the death penalty, and this publicity, along with the continued interest in the Loeb-Leopold decision, filled the theatre to capacity. As in all of the Darrow debates during the 1920s, this afternoon's entertainment was not free; tickets for the Darrow-Talley clash ranged in price from $1.65 to $4.40, depending upon how close one sat to the stage. [23] While no financial statement was released after the conclusion of the debate, it appears most probable that the League for Public Discussion was able to realize a profit from the encounter. Since this was during the time that Darrow often debated for minimal expense money, it also appears probable that little money was spent on fees for the participants. Thus, with the gate receipts and with the later publication of the debaters' speeches by the Haldeman-Julius Company, the League for Public Discussion, holder of the debate's copyright, probably realized a profit of several thousands of dollars.

Unlike contemporary intercollegiate debate, the public forum debates of the 1920s included more formal trappings and the active involvement of other people besides the debaters. Whereas a modern debate consists of just the debaters and the judges, the public debates of the 1920s also included at least one "debate chairman," whose purpose was to introduce the debaters and to keep the program moving. The Darrow-Talley debate had three people involved in the program besides the debaters: an individual from the League for Public Discussion who introduced the "temporary chairman" of the debate whose purpose, in turn, was to introduce the "permanent chairman" of the debate. This third person, finally, was responsible for the setting forth of the topic for debate and for the introduction of the debaters. Thus, a member of the audience could expect to be regaled by this procession of people for nearly half an hour before the debate actually began.

Mr. Benjamin A. Javits of the League for Public Discussion opened the afternoon's festivities with a simple three-line introduction of the debate's temporary chairman, Lewis E. Lawes. Theoretically, one would hope or expect that an individual filling a chairperson's role would attempt to demonstrate impartiality vis-a-vis the debate topic. However, Lawes, warden of Sing Sing Prison, was an outspoken critic of capital punishment, and this bias was quite apparent during his opening presentation. Although Lawes admitted that it was his responsibility to remain impartial, he continued to suggest that capital punishment did not deter crime and that it was the poor man in society who fell prey to the law and the exercise of the death penalty:

Now, this subject is something worthy of all men and women thinking about. We find in Rhode Island (a small state, but with no capital punishment) a high percentage of foreigners and yet a low percentage of murders. We find that throughout Europe it is much lower than we find it here.

Is it true that a poor man always goes? Is it true that a rich man never goes? I don't mean to imply by that that the judge or that the jury is anything but fair. But one who has money is able to hire counsel and able to present his case so much better. In

any event, try and find someone who had money who has gone.[24]

After concluding these clearly prejudicial remarks, Lawes then introduced the permanent chairman of the debate, famous constitutional lawyer Louis Marshall. Quite appropriately Marshall set the scene for the debate by quickly sketching a brief history of the use of capital punishment from ancient Greece to the era of the 1920s. However, like Warden Lawes, Marshall allowed his bias to creep into his presentation by suggesting that if one possessed genuine humane qualities and were concerned with a sympathetic understanding of all human conduct, then one would desire the abolition of capital punishment:

The subject is not an easy one. If we follow our sympathetic hearts, if we really act according to the natural impulses of a human being, we would be all apt to say that capital punishment should be abolished.[25]

After concluding these remarks, Marshall outlined the procedure that was to be followed in the debate itself:

The argument will be opened by Judge Talley in an address which will last for thirty-five minutes. Mr. Darrow will follow and will have forty minutes for his opening speech; Judge Talley will follow with a rebuttal which will occupy twenty minutes; and Mr. Darrow will close with a speech of fifteen minutes. Each therefore having fifty-five minutes allotted to him.[26]

Thus, after nearly thirty minutes of preliminaries, the Darrow-Talley debate was allowed to begin.

Judge Talley's Argumentation and Strategy

Throughout the course of his thirty-five minute constructive speech, Judge Talley utilized seven major lines of argumentation in support of the position that capital punishment was a wise public policy (see Table I). As noted previously, the specific subject of debate ("Is Capital Punishment A Wise Public Policy?") entailed the consideration of a value-oriented proposition, and such a proposition often provides difficulty in handling issues within a debate. Since the subject itself is "loaded" with a term that implies some sort of value dimension—in this case, what is a "wise" public policy—it often creates the unhappy situation of debaters not clashing on the issues because their individual value dimensions differ.[27] Thus, to allow for clash, the value dimension must be defined.

Judge Talley began his presentation with a definition of what would constitute a wise public policy: " . . . that which is reasonably calculated to accomplish the end which is sought."[28] Since it was contended that the desired results of capital punishment would be the elimination of wanton, premeditated murder, Talley further limited the debate to a consideration of capital punishment *vis-a-vis* the commission of murder:

. . . *all we need to concern ourselves with this afternoon is the question of the wisdom and the expediency and the utility of the state exercising the right to put to death one guilty of the crime of murder.*[29]

Therefore, by definition and topic limitation, the proper scope of the debate entailed argument centering upon the expediency and utility of capital punishment in cases of homicide. Treason, rape, kidnapping, and other felonious crimes were not to fall within the penumbra of the debate. As the affirmative spokesman on the proposition, Judge Talley possessed the right to so limit the debate, and such limitation is generally a solid

strategic maneuver because it forces the opponent to argue on one's predetermined territory.[30]

With the topic so defined and limited, Talley began his specific argumentation, proceeding from several general lines of thought to more specific arguments concerning the basic issue of capital punishment itself. First, he contended that the state had the right to execute those who had violated the law:

. . . *capital punishment is the right exercised by the state to put to death one who has violated that law of the state which says, 'Thou shalt not kill,' that right to kill in self-defense . . . .*

Does anyone dispute the right of a nation to kill in the protection of its citizens? Why should the right of any state be questioned when it seeks to protect its citizens . . . against unjust aggression?[31]

The strategic strength of this argument lies in its philosophical impact for the remainder of the arguments. If Talley was able to create the agreement that the state had the right to kill, then the remainder of the debate would, of necessity, be limited to the effectiveness of capital punishment. If no such agreement were reached, then it is quite possible that the entirety of the debate would center on this general moral and ethical issue, thereby eliminating discussion of the utilitarian aspects of capital punishment. As it turned out, Darrow did not dispute the state's right to kill, and this subject became a noncontended moot issue. Talley's argument was an attempt to preempt a philosophical position that Darrow chose not to defend.

From this point, Talley further limited the discussion by noting that capital punishment was utilized only against those who have been adjudged guilty of premeditated murder:

Table I   Major Arguments in the Darrow-Talley Debate

Alfred J. Talley	Clarence Darrow
The state has the right to execute in self-defense	(Admitted)
Capital punishment is used only in cases of premeditated murder	No one knows what premeditation is
Every man knows that it is wrong to kill	Every man desires killing
The criminal defendant can be provided with free counsel	The poor and weak are the victims of the law
Modern imprisonment is too easy on the prisoner	Must we torture a man in prison?
Capital punishment is needed to enforce the laws	To create respect for the law, the state should not kill
Capital punishment is a deterrent to crime	Capital punishment is not a deterrent to crime; why not make punishment truly terrible?
War had no influence upon the increase in crime	War has increased lawlessness
Advocates of capital punishment abhor killing	Advocates of capital punishment love killing
	Statistics are not relevant to a consideration of capital punishment
Men are responsible for their acts	No one can measure out justice

. . . *the only kind of homicide that is punishable by death is what we designate as murder in the first degree. And that is the killing of a human being–which is neither excusable or justifiable, and which follows deliberation and premeditation upon the part of the killer.* [32]

This argument served to demonstrate that capital punishment was not wantonly used by the authorities of the state to snuff out the lives of many convicted felons. Instead, the use of capital punishment was quite carefully circumscribed to affect only those convicted of premeditated murder. While it is impossible to ascertain the specific reason as to why this argument was included by Talley, it did serve to create the impression that capital punishment

was utilized in only the most extreme circumstances. It is quite possible that Talley, being familiar with Darrow's arguments in the Loeb-Leopold case, geared this argument to preempt the impression that capital punishment was widely used by a bloodthirsty criminal justice system, an impression clearly created by Darrow in the Chicago trial two months before. Whatever the reason for the argument, Darrow did dispute it and attempted to claim that advocates of capital punishment enjoyed the thrill of killing.

Talley's third argument was also general in nature, wherein he claimed that every man knew that it was wrong to kill:

In the heart of every man is written the law, "Thou shalt not kill.' Upon the statute books of every civilized community is written the law, 'Thou shalt not kill.' And no one offends that precept through ignorance. It is fundamental that every man knows it is wrong and illegal to take the life of another man.[33]

The point of this argument was that the prohibition against the commission of homicide was not merely a governmental ban upon such activity. Every man himself, morally and ethically, knew that it was wrong to commit murder, that it was wrong to kill. Thus, the massive weight of collective society could be brought against the individual murderer who transgressed against not only the dictates of law but also the dictates of civilized humanity. While this particular argument might seem to be of minimal significance, it should be pointed out that this argument places the individual murderer outside the mainstream of organized society and rationalizes the use of an extreme penalty like capital punishment against the transgressor. Therefore, the murderer is seen as a societal aberration, a man for whom compassion is not justified. This point was hotly contested by Darrow during his constructive speech.

Talley's next two arguments were concerned with the rights of the accused prisoner and convicted felon. First, he considered what alternative existed to the exercise of capital punishment and claimed that imprisonment was not an adequate replacement. Instead of punishment, prisons provided a lifestyle that was luxurious in relation to those living on the "outside":

If you happen to kill in the State of New York, you will be provided with a moving picture show every night of the week, and at various times during the season prominent Broadway stars will bring up their companies and their paraphernalia for your entertainment. Your less fortunate brother, who has respected the law, must pay for that entertainment in

the theaters of Broadway. But you, a ward of the state, will be provided with these things without the necessity of paying for them at all.[34]

Therefore, because of this "luxurious" living, imprisonment was not an adequate replacement for capital punishment. Why should a man, convicted of the premeditated murder of another, be allowed to enjoy the movies at the expense of law-abiding society? It should be noted that Talley's unhappiness with the screening of motion pictures at Sing Sing Prison provided Darrow with several moments of sarcastic humorous response. It should also be noted that this particular argument was an extension of the complaint issued by Talley in his news release of September 22.[35]

Conjoined with the above argument was Talley's contention that the accused murderer would be provided with free defense counsel if he was unable to afford one. The point of this one-sentence position was to deny the concept that the poor and weak serve as the cannon fodder for the American criminal justice system. Darrow had often publicly claimed that people served time in prison and forfeited their lives at the gallows because of the lack of adequate defense counsel. It is quite possible that, again, Talley attempted to preempt an expected argument from Darrow. After all, Warden Lawes had raised this particular issue in his rather biased presentation.

With over one-half of his speaking time dissipated, Talley finally turned to the specific question of the expediency and the utility of capital punishment. In the time remaining to him, he was able to crystallize two major arguments. First, he contended that capital punishment was needed to enforce the laws:

Those who would seek to take away from the state the power to impose capital punishment seek to despoil the symbol of justice . . . they would take from her hand the sword, without which the other symbols would be meaningless things. For if justice has not the right to enforce her edicts and her mandates, then her laws may be lost upon a senseless people. [36]

The impact of this enforcement argument was provided by a second interrelated argument—that capital punishment was effective because it served to deter crime:

. . . I say that the only thing the criminal fears is the penalty of death that will follow his crime. And I need not read that in any book or any essay or any treatise. That is my experience of more than twenty-five years. [37]

Therefore, because capital punishment is the only penalty that can cause an individual to steer clear of criminal actions and because capital punishment is the only penalty that provides sufficient power to uphold the law, then capital punishment should be viewed as a wise public policy for its accrual of two major goals within the operation of organized society.

Since the most compelling argument in support of the proposition centered upon the issue of deterrence, the type of reasoning and evidence in substantiation of the argument merits consideration. Talley provided no factual or opinionated support for his assertion; his contention that capital punishment deterred criminal activity was based entirely upon his own experience. In addition, Talley merely rejected the works of "Bocalley and Lombroso and Lawes and other men" who had concluded that capital punishment was not a deterrent to crime, without explaining or justifying their rejection. The totality of support for his position came from his own experience exclusively.

Talley's support for his deterrence argument was also based upon an interesting effect-to-cause *post hoc* bit of reasoning:

Who can say, and substantiate his assertion, that in this country of ours, shamed with ten thousand murders in every twelve months–who can say, with that criminal tendency upon the part of the American people, that stigmatizes us as to the most lawless nation on the face of the earth–who can say that, with murder in the heart of so many of our people, the number would not be twice as great or three times as great if death, which is still the king of terrors (more to the criminal than to the righteous man), were not maintained as the penalty for an unlawful killing? [38]

The interesting part of this reasoning is that one must assume that capital punishment is, in fact, a deterrent to crime before the point suggested by Talley can be accepted. That is, one must accept the concept of deterrence to be able to agree that the number of murders would be two or three times greater without capital punishment. This was the entirety of the reasoning and evidence in support of Judge Talley's final major argument in his constructive speech. The remainder of his speaking time was spent in a boring recitation of statistics indicating that crime was on the increase throughout the United States. With the final statement that he would favor the abolition of capital punishment "when the murderers of the country abolish its necessity," Talley closed his initial presentation and turned the floor over to Darrow.

Clarence Darrow's Argumentation and Strategy

As the spokesman for the negative position within this debate, Clarence Darrow had the responsibility of dealing directly with the major

31

arguments advanced by Judge Talley as well as the option of presenting any additional arguments that he considered relevant to the consideration of the debate proposition. Darrow upheld his responsibility by clashing with every major argument of Talley's, although the organization that was followed left a bit to be desired.

Instead of handling each argument in its order within the initial presentation, Darrow chose to follow a relatively haphazard arrangement of refutation that could have thoroughly confused the audience had Judge Talley's speech been less well-organized. As a point of comparison, Darrow's constructive speech in the debate with Talley was similar to his final plea in the Loeb-Leopold case in its rather free-wheeling organization of materials. One who has read either speech would realize that Darrow suffered from a lack of organization, yet the final meaning and impact of the combined arguments are quite clear. It may well be that the simplicity of style in the usage of language overcame this lack of organization. Whatever the case, one reading or listening to Darrow's constructive speech would find it difficult to sense any sort of organizational framework within the presentation of material. For this reason, this writer has decided to describe Darrow's major arguments by aligning them with the argumentative substructure laid out by Talley.

As to Talley's contention that the state possessed the right to kill in self-defense, Darrow acknowledged agreement. However, it is significant that this concurrence was based upon a very negative view of the use of power:

I don't want to dispute with him the right of the state to kill people. Of course, they have got a right to kill them. That is

about all we do. The great industry of the world for four long years was killing. They have got a right to kill, of course. That is, they have got the power. And you have got a right to do what you get away with. The words power and right, so far as this is concerned, mean exactly the same thing. [39]

Thus, instead of granting the state a moral or ethical right to execute criminals, Darrow chose to suggest that "might makes right," thereby dropping the choice of presenting a philosophical indictment of Talley's position. Whether Darrow chose not to argue this point because he lacked interest in it or because he considered it to be insignificant within the context of the debate is not known. The right of the state to kill became an admitted issue.

Second, Darrow did choose to contest Talley's position that capital punishment is utilized only in cases of premeditated murder. His argument was that no one knew what actually constituted premeditation:

What does any judge know about premeditation? What does anybody know about it? How many people are there in this world that can premeditate on anything? I will take out the 'pre' and say how many people are there that can meditate? [40]

The point of this argument was that the utilization of capital punishment was based upon an ill-defined, imprecise concept within the criminal law that precluded an absolute assurance that such a factor actually existed. Therefore, capital punishment was based upon something that, for all intents and purposes, did not exist:

How long does it take the angry man for his passions to cool when he is in the presence of the thing that angers him? There never was a premeditated murder in any sense of psychology or science.

There are planned murders–planned, yes–but back of every murder and back of every human act are sufficient causes that move the human machine beyond their control. [41]

Because of these hidden motivations, the concept of premeditation is not operationally valid, thus there is no rationale for capital punishment.

A great deal of Talley's philosophical support for his position sprang from the contention that, inherently, man knew that it was wrong to take the life of another human being. Darrow mixed humor and innuendo in refuting Talley's argument:

. . . I deny his statement that every man's heart tells him it is wrong to kill. I think every man's heart desires killing. Personally, I never killed anybody that I know of. But I have had a great deal of satisfaction now and then reading obituary notices, and I used to delight, with the rest of my hundred percent patriotic friends, when I saw ten or fifteen thousand Germans being killed in a day.

Everybody loves killing. Some of them think it is too messy for them. Every human being that believes in capital punishment loves killing, and the only reason they believe in capital punishment is because they get a kick out of it. [42]

Darrow was unable to substantiate this argument beyond presenting his own experiential conclusions; Talley was also unable to present any factual or experimentally based evidence for his position. This argument appealed solely to the attitudinal predispositions to be found within the members of the audience.

It should be remembered that Judge Talley's objection to the substitution of imprisonment for capital punishment was that imprisonment was too luxurious for the prisoner, that the prisoner led a better life in confinement than those who obeyed the laws. Darrow chose to attack this argument by reducing it to the point of absurdity, as the following extract aptly demonstrates:

Is there any reason for torturing someone who happens to be in prison? Is there any reason why an actor or even an actress might not go there and sing? There is no objection to a preacher going there. Why not give him a little pleasure?

And you can take your meals out! Now, some of you might not have noticed that I walked over and asked the Warden [Lewis E. Lawes of Sing Sing] about it. The reason I did that is because I am stopping over here at the Belmont and I didn't know but I'd rather go up and board with him. Why, I wonder if the judge ever took the pains to go up there. I will tell you. I have had some experience with people that know them pretty well. I never saw a man who wanted to go to prison, even to see the movies. [43]

By reducing Talley's argument to the point of absurdity, Darrow attempted to deny the compelling significance of the judge's objections to life imprisonment as the alternative to capital punishment. Instead of directly refuting Talley's indictments of prisons, Darrow poked fun at the argument, causing the audience members to refute Talley with their own laughter. The transcriber recorded ten separate instances of audience laughter while Darrow presented this five-minute piece of implied refutation.

Darrow also engaged in a similar strategy in dealing with the contention that all criminal defendants were provided with able defense counsel. Besides denying that contention, Darrow also tried to get the audience to laugh Talley's argument out of the theatre:

Now, I don't know how injustice is administered in New York. I just know about Chicago. But I am glad to learn from the gentleman that if a man is so poor in New York that he can't hire a

*lawyer, that he has a first-class lawyer
appointed to defend him. Don't take a
chance and go out and kill anybody on the
statement made by my friend . . . no
court ever interferes with a good lawyer's
business by calling him in and compelling
him to give his time. They have been
lawyers too recently themselves to ever
work a trick like that on a lawyer.*[44]

Although the audience did laugh in
response to Darrow's humor, the
situation that existed in relation to
the preceding argument did not
repeat itself. This time, Talley did not
drop his contention but, rather,
extended it through the rebuttal
period with, it must be added, the
assistance of Louis Marshall, whose
introduction to the rebuttal period
was highlighted by his insistence that
Darrow's argument was incorrect.[45]
Darrow chose to repeat his belief that
it was the judge and Mr. Marshall
who were incorrect.

This led to a consideration of Talley's
final two arguments that bore directly
upon the expediency and utility of
capital punishment. As to the
argument that the death penalty was
needed to give force to the nation's
laws, Darrow responded that, in
practice, capital punishment was
counterproductive in that it created a
bad example for the people:

*We teach people to kill, and the state is
the one that teaches them. If a state
wishes that its citizens respect human
life, then the state should stop killing. It
can be done in no other way . . . .*[46]

This argument is based upon the
"monkey see, monkey do" concept
of causality that is, at best, tenuous.
Darrow was unable to provide any
meaningful evidence or analysis to
support this causal argument,
whereas Talley was able to argue the
point of utility. If one were opposed
to killing on principle, Darrow's
argument would seem quite sound; if
one were a staunch advocate of "law

and order," Talley's argument would
seem more sound.

Finally, Darrow dealt with the
argument that capital punishment
was a societal necessity to serve as a
deterrent to crime. Instead of blasting
Talley's position with a plethora of
statistics indicating that the homicide
rate was not affected by the presence
of capital punishment, Darrow
issued only a broad, fleeting swipe at
Talley's causal argument:

*I might just observe in passing that in all
of these states where the mortality by
homicide is great, they have capital
punishment and always have had it. A
logical man, when he found out that the
death rate increased under capital
punishment, would suggest some other
way of dealing with it.*[47]

Later on during his constructive
speech, Darrow returned to the
question of deterrence and utilized
illustration to argue that capital
punishment is not an effective
before-the-fact check on crime:

*Can you imagine a woman following a
man around with a pistol to kill him that
would stop if you said, 'Oh, you will be
hanged!' Nothing doing—not if the world
was coming to an end! Can you imagine a
man doing it? They think of it
afterwards, but not before. They come
from acts like burglary and robbery. A
man goes out to rob or to burglarize.
Somebody catches him or stops him or
recognizes him, and he kills to save
himself. Do you suppose there was ever a
burglar or robber since the world began
who would not kill to save himself? Is
there anybody who wouldn't? It doesn't
make any difference who . . . . Anyone
would do it.*[48]

However, it must be noted that
Darrow decided to go one step
beyond the mere refutation of the
point of deterrence. He decided to
extend logically Talley's argument
and then reduce it to absurdity:

34

*If you want to get rid of killings by
hanging people or electrocuting them
because these are so terrible, why not
make a punishment that is terrible? This
isn't so much. It lasts but a short time.
There is no physical torture in it. Why
not boil them in oil, as they used to do?
Why not burn them at the
stake? . . . Those were the good old
days in which the judge should have held
court. Glorious days, when you could kill
them by the million because they
worshipped God in a different way from
that which the state provided, or when
you could kill old women for
witchcraft! . . . Those were the
glorious days of capital
punishment . . . . Why, our capital
punishment isn't worth talking about so
far as its being a preventive is
concerned.* [49]

The raucous audience response to
this extension of argument was
overwhelming; Talley dropped the
argument of deterrence after being
placed in the company of
witch-burners.

Darrow vs. Talley—An Evaluation

The program that had been printed
for distribution to the debate
audience contained a judging ballot,
wherein each member of the
audience was asked to vote as to who
had won the Darrow-Talley clash. [50]
Since Darrow consistently objected to
the rendering of a decision at the
conclusion of a debate, the audience
was requested to return the ballots to
the League for Public Discussion by
mail. The results of this balloting
were never made public. However, if
overt audience reaction was a valid
indication of sentiment, then it is
clear from the transcript of the debate
that Darrow held the upper hand; yet
such a conclusion is purely
speculative and is not based upon
reliable data.

Rendering a decision in the
Darrow-Talley debate would be quite
difficult because of the lack of
adequate extension of the major lines
of argument by both debaters. Talley
utilized seven major arguments in his
constructive speech, but he dropped
six of them in his rebuttal. The only
argument that he pulled through the
debate was the peripheral argument
that criminal defendants are
provided with free counsel if they are
unable to afford one of their own
choice. Talley failed to respond to
Darrow's arguments in refutation of
the initial affirmative presentation.

Darrow did not fare much better.
Like Talley, he dropped the vast
majority of his constructive
arguments, extending only those two
arguments dealing with the rights of
criminal defendants and the
nondeterrence of capital
punishment. Darrow allowed Talley
to drop his substructure without
saying a word about it. If it was
Darrow's strategy to utilize humor
and invective to force Talley to drop
the essential arguments within his
case, then he overwhelmingly
succeeded. If he desired to promote a
high-level discussion on the salient
issues inherent within capital
punishment, then his style of
refutation abrogated the achievement
of that goal. Because Talley did drop
his substructure and failed to respond
to the specifics of Darrow's
refutation, Darrow was able to carry
the major lines of argument and
should be awarded the decision in
this debate.

Some analysis of the arguments
utilized by both debaters seems
warranted. First, Talley must be
chastised for his failure to maintain
his own definition of terms. He
defined a wise public policy as one
that "is reasonably calculated to
accomplish the end which is sought,"
but five of his seven arguments had
absolutely nothing to do with this
concept of expediency and utility.
The two arguments that were
pertinent to this definition—the need

35

for capital punishment to enforce the laws and to deter crime—were developed in such a hurried and shallow manner as to negate their impact. Both arguments were supported only by Talley's experience as an attorney and judge, and he openly spurned counterarguments without justifying their rejection. In short, Talley wasted his time on peripheral arguments and failed to develop those issues that had a direct bearing upon the topic under discussion. His was a very weak case indeed.

Clarence Darrow's refutation also was none too strong. Like Talley, he failed to support his major arguments with any substantial amount of factual or opinionated evidence, preferring instead to assert contentions that were based upon his experience as a defense attorney. Thus, a member of the audience would be forced to decide the issues upon the basis of assertions of two men, with no additional information available. Also, while it is true that it is the responsibility of the negative speaker to refute the arguments of the affirmative, it was not Darrow's responsibility to waste as much time with those peripheral arguments as Talley had. As an experienced forensic advocate, Darrow should have clearly seen that the crux of the debate lay in Talley's final two arguments. However, he wasted most of his time on the first peripheral arguments and then was only able to deal with the crucial issues in a slipshod manner. Darrow's case would have been greatly improved had he quickly touched upon Talley's initial five arguments and then concentrated the remainder of his attention upon the final two arguments. It would have made the Darrow victory much clearer to the audience.

One other aspect of the debate should be considered. The inherent difficulty with a value-oriented debate proposition is that it requires a careful aligning of the debaters' value dimensions to assure adequate clash on the issues. Despite the fact that Talley attempted such an alignment, the rebuttal periods made it quite clear that the debaters were in two different philosophical worlds. Whereas Talley's major concern was for the victims of crime,[51] Darrow's major concern was with the lot of every man, the criminal as well as the victim.[52] This fundamental difference in philosophy caused the debaters to talk about varying aspects of the same basic issues. Because of this difference, Darrow won the debate by default.

Footnotes

1. See the *New York Times*, June 30, 1972, pp. 1 and 14; and the *Washington Post*, June 30, 1972, pp. A1 and A12. Also, see *Time* (March 25, 1974), p. 10.

2. For an excellent description of the various forms of capital punishment utilized in man's recorded history, see George V. Bishop, *Executions: The Legal Ways of Death* (Los Angeles, 1965).

3. Marquis Beccaria, "Of the Punishment of Death," in *The Opinions of Different Authors upon the Punishment of Death*, edited by Basil Montagu (London, 1816), p. 25.

4. James Avery Joyce, *Capital Punishment* (New York, 1961), p. 268; and the *New York Times*, June 20, 1972, p. 14.

5. Irving Stone, *Clarence Darrow For the Defense* (Garden City, 1941), pp. 29-30. Darrow admitted the influence of Altgeld upon his life in his autobiography, *The Story of My Life* (New York, 1932), p. 41, but he incorrectly titled Altgeld's work as *Our Penal Code and Its Victims*.

6. Darrow, *The Story of My Life*, p. 349. This same argument was used in the defense of Richard Loeb and Nathan Leopold; see Arthur Weinberg, ed., *Attorney for the Damned* (New York, 1957), pp. 16-88.

7. John Peter Altgeld, *Our Penal Machinery and Its Victims*, in *Live Questions* (Chicago, 1899), p. 31.

8. Arthur Garfield Hays, *City Lawyer* (New York, 1942), p. 210.

9. Clarence Darrow, "The Human Being's World," in *A Preface to the Universe*, edited by Baker Brownell (New York, 1929), pp. 77-79. See also, Clarence Darrow, "The Futility of the Death Penalty," *Forum*, LXXX (September, 1928), pp. 330-331.

10. Altgeld, p. 16.

11. John Peter Altgeld, "General Message on the Assembly of the Legislature," in *Live Questions* (Chicago, 1899, p. 908.

12. The *New York Times*, March 14, 1938, p. 15.

13. The *New York Times*, February 17, 1929, p. 24.

14. Ray Ginger, *Altgeld's America* (New York, 1958), p. 347.

15. Darrow, *The Story of My Life*, pp. 230-236.

16. The pressures placed upon Judge Caverly are explored by Francis X. Busch, *Prisoners at the Bar* (New York, 1952).

17. *Ibid.*, p. 162. See also, the *New York Times*, September 11, 1924, pp. 1-2.

18. The *New York Times*, September 11, 1924, p. 22.

19. The *New York Times*, September 22, 1924, p. 21.

20. The *New York Times*, September 23, 1924, p. 25.

21. The League for Public Discussion was a private organization that sponsored many public forum discussions throughout the New York metropolitan area during the 1920s. Available information indicates that this organization was headquartered at 500 Fifth Avenue in New York and ceased activities *circa* 1930.

22. Arthur Weinberg has confused the date of this debate with the date of Talley's "anti-criminal coddling" statement in the *New York Times*. Weinberg's work has the debate take place over one month before it actually occurred. See Arthur Weinberg, ed., *Attorney for the Damned* (New York, 1957), p. 89.

23. The *New York Times*, October 27, 1924, p. 40.

24. Clarence Darrow and Alfred J. Talley, *Debate on Capital Punishment* (Girard, 1924), p. 9.

25. *Ibid.*, p. 12.

26. *Ibid.*, p. 14.

27. For an excellent discussion of the difficulties involved in a proposition of value, see Douglas Ehninger and Wayne Brockriede, *Decision By Debate* (New York, 1963), pp. 221-223.

28. Darrow and Talley, p. 16.

29. *Ibid.*, p. 17.

30. The strategic advantage of a prompt and carefully planned definition of terms is discussed by Austin J. Freeley, *Argumentation and Debate*, third edition (Belmont, 1971), pp. 44-46.

[31] Darrow and Talley, pp. 16 and 22.

[32] *Ibid.*, p. 17.

[33] *Ibid.*, p. 18.

[34] *Ibid.*, pp. 20-21.

[35] The *New York Times*, September 23, 1924, p. 25.

[36] Darrow and Talley, pp. 22-23.

[37] *Ibid.*, p. 23.

[38] *Ibid.*, p. 24.

[39] *Ibid.*, p. 32.

[40] *Ibid.*, pp. 35-36.

[41] *Ibid.*, p. 36.

[42] *Ibid.*, pp. 28-29.

[43] *Ibid.*, pp. 38-39.

[44] *Ibid.*, pp. 34-35.

[45] *Ibid.*, p. 45.

[46] *Ibid.*, p. 31.

[47] *Ibid.*, p. 29.

[48] *Ibid.*, pp. 42-43.

[49] *Ibid.*, p. 33.

[50] The *New York Times*, October 27, 1924, p. 40.

[51] Darrow and Talley, pp. 51-52.

[52] *Ibid.*, p. 61.

Chapter Four

Prohibition

After one year from the ratification of this article, the manufacture, sale, or transportation of intoxicating liquors within, the importation thereof into, or the exportation thereof from the United States and all territory subject to the jurisdiction thereof for beverage purposes is hereby prohibited. [1]

. . . with the great social awakening that occurred after 1900, welfare workers, social scientists, and other middle-class Americans became concerned as never before with the problems of disease, crime, poverty, vice, and suffering, and the extent to which these were caused by alcohol. [2]

The ratification of the foregoing Eighteenth Amendment to the United States Constitution was completed in January 1919. One year later, the national Prohibition against the use of alcoholic beverages was implemented, and the American people were to begin a thirteen-year period in the "noble experiment" against the forces of Demon Rum. As with all such similar social legislation, the policy of Prohibition did not come into existence overnight. Years of planning and preparation were necessary to create the support for and acceptance of a national policy that was negative in its method while, supposedly, positive in its consequences.

The Prohibition Movement

The movement for a national prohibition against the use of alcoholic beverages stemmed, in large part, from the social goals of the progressive movement of the early twentieth century. At that time, there was an increased concern with the various ills that continued to plague society, particularly crime and poverty, and with the relationship of these evils with the alcoholic beverage traffic:

Progressives saw that there was an undeniable link between alcohol and the major social ills, and, more importantly, it was seen that the liquor industry itself was a crucial part of the perceived corruptness of government at the local and state levels:

The progressive movement sided with the prohibitionists in trying to get rid of the corrupt city machines and the vice areas based on the saloons. [3]

Since it was a common practice for the alcoholic beverage industry to intervene directly in the practices of government to secure beneficial regulatory practices and enforcement, the progressive movement tended to support prohibition organizations such as the Anti-Saloon League and the Women's Christian Temperance Union in the effort to break this corrupt influence upon local government.

Therefore, the progressive movement coincided with the Prohibition movement because of the desire to uplift society and to improve the lot of the common man. Since it was believed that the alcoholic beverage industry was nothing more than another conglomerate monopoly that exploited the poor common man of American society, progressives supported the call for a national prohibition against alcohol to utilize "the power of government as a positive instrument of reform."[4] As Timberlake has noted, progressive support of national Prohibition was based upon the same moral idealism that characterized the other desired reforms of the progressive movement.[5]

Besides having the support and overt assistance of the progressives, the Prohibition movement also had the support of the adherents to the Social Gospel of the early 1900s. The rationale for this religious support is best explained by examining the philosophical base upon which the Social Gospel operated. Basically, as defined by Paul Carter, the Social Gospel preached that "men are obliged to act directly upon the social order and work for its reconstruction."[6] Thus, since man was responsible for the care and uplifting of his fellow man, it was only natural that the adherents of the Social Gospel supported those ventures that promised to improve the condition of mankind. Prohibitionists claimed that the elimination of the alcoholic beverage traffic would be a monumental step in the overall betterment of man's life on earth. This claim of positive societal consequences was illustrated by Robert A. Woods of Boston's South End House in 1919:

. . . prohibition was going to stimulate business activity; raise the standard of living; foster sound, productive labor organizations; unleash vast suppressed human potentialities; and elevate the moral sense of the plain people.[7]

With such perceived benefits, the Social Gospel movement adopted the tenet of national prohibition as a part of its work in the reconstruction of society. By 1920, with the exception of the Protestant Episcopal Churches, "all the churches which had been permeated by the Social Gospel were also officially committed to Prohibition."[8]

One other factor that bore upon the support for Prohibition needs to be mentioned. As documented in Chapter Two, the 1920s were an era of ideological and philosophical hostility between the rural and urban segments of the American nation because of the interplay of numerous factors. One of the largest obstacles preventing a rural-urban rapprochement was created by the differing attitudes toward national prohibition: the rural areas supported it; the urban areas opposed it.

Kirschner has suggested that the major reason underlying rural support for Prohibition was the desire to take revenge on the urban areas for their transgressions against the morality and lifestyle of the past.[9] In short, the rural areas used Prohibition as an instrument of punishment against the urbanites:

Ruralites in the Midwest entered the 1920s with clear ideas about where the world was going wrong and why, but they were not of one mind about how to correct it . . . . Prohibition . . . was the rural cause, the one nationwide symbol of rural opposition to everything that was wrong in America.[10]

Whether one accepts Kirschner's interpretation is of no great importance to this study. What is important is that there was a definite rural-urban split on the issue of Prohibition. The native American agrarian supported the call for a strict ban against the use of alcoholic beverages, while the cosmopolite urban areas opposed Prohibition from the start. This split became more pronounced during the 1920s when there was a national effort to enforce the Eighteenth Amendment.

Thus, the Prohibition movement drew its initial support from the members of the progressive movement and the Social Gospel, as well as from the rural areas of the American nation. By the time of America's entry into the First World War, the efforts of these groups had caused the majority of the American people to become "dry," because various local-option statutes had implemented the ban against alcohol in over sixty percent of the nation's counties. The First World War provided the final impetus to make Prohibition a firm, national policy.

The Impetus of the First World War

As the United States entered the First World War, the forces advocating a national prohibition against alcohol possessed the advantage of superior organization and communication. Prohibitionists had, during the preceding twenty years, created an impressive national network of information-gathering and diffusion that had effectively molded public opinion against the liquor industry. Led by Wayne B. Wheeler of the Anti-Saloon League, the advocates of Prohibition possessed the strategic advantage of being on the offensive against the evils of alcohol, while the opponents of temperance were only loosely organized in support of the unsavory practices of the liquor industry.

However, despite the existence of this organizational and strategic disparity, the adoption of an amendment to the United States Constitution that would severely limit the use of alcohol seemed remote. Although it might be accepted that the liquor industry had engaged in illegal and unethical governmental practices and that alcohol was a negative element in the functioning of society, there would always exist those individuals who would oppose the extension of federal governmental authority into areas of social policy. The support of these individuals, termed the "psychologically tolerant" by Andrew Sinclair, was necessary in order to create a national policy of prohibition against alcohol.[11] This support was created by American involvement in the First World War, because the necessity for the conservation of grain and other such liquor-producing materials, as well as the wartime hysteria against most products of foreign origin, made the concept of national prohibition more acceptable to most Americans:

The war diverted the attention of those who might have objected to the bone-dry program: with the very existence of the nation at stake, the future status of alcohol seemed a trifling matter. The war accustomed the country to drastic legislation conferring new and wide powers upon the federal government. It necessitated the saving of food and thus commended Prohibition to the patriotic as a grain-saving measure. It turned public opinion against everything German—and many of the big brewers and distillers were of German origin. The war also brought with it a mood of Spartan idealism of which the Eighteenth Amendment was a natural expression.[12]

Thus, the United States Congress voted favorably upon the proposed policy of national prohibition in 1917; the required three-fourths of the state legislatures ratified the constitutional amendment by January 1919. To enforce the program, Congress adopted, over President Wilson's veto, the Volstead Act that was designed to provide the necessary financial and manpower material to implement the Eighteenth Amendment. The "noble experiment" began in January 1920.

41

Prohibition During the 1920s

Aided by the reform-oriented progressive movement, strengthened by the arguments provided by various social scientists, and given a final forward thrust by national necessities brought on by the First World War, Prohibition appeared to enjoy massive national support at the time of its implementation. However, the era of the 1920s marked a distinct change in the philosophy underlying Prohibition, and it was this change that caused Prohibition to become the major failure in national social policy during the twentieth century.

It must be remembered that the early movement for a policy of national prohibition looked upon the user of alcohol as an unfortunate tool of the despicable and contemptible liquor industry. Both philosophically and rhetorically, the devil term for highest condemnation of the early Prohibitionists was "the liquor industry."[13] It was this industry that was responsible for the corruption of individuals and governmental practices; early Prohibitionists sought to secure controls over the excesses of the liquor industry. However, Prohibition during the 1920s viewed matters much differently. By 1920 the "devil" was no longer the liquor industry; the user of alcoholic beverages became the focus of contempt as the evil became more personified.

This shift in emphasis became crucial to the ultimate lack of success that so symbolized Prohibition. By changing the "devil" from the liquor industry to the individual consumer, Prohibition lost the support of those people who were needed to make the national policy successful:

The tragedy of the Prohibition movement was that it lost the support of moderates and liberals and became a revolutionary faction . . . [it] mistook the support of moderates against the saloon for their support in banning liquor altogether . . . the drys alienated the support of the psychologically tolerant.[14]

As Paul Carter has noted, "The humanitarian concern for the drunkard as victim was replaced by righteous indignation at the drunkard as criminal," and this psychological shift caused the loss of support for national Prohibition.[15]

In addition, it should also be noted that the excesses of the implementation of the Eighteenth Amendment caused a decline in the support for Prohibition. Proposals to put toxic poisons in industrial alcohol to check the circumvention of the law created a negative public response. While many people might agree that a country without alcohol was a positive ideal, the idea of poisoning violators of the law without benefit of judge or jury was another concept altogether. Such proposals tended to harm the cause of Prohibition. Also, the Volstead Act, the Eighteenth Amendment's enforcing mechanism, contained provisions that were of no benefit to Prohibition's image. For example, the Volstead Act outlawed goods that contained in excess of one-half of one per cent of alcohol, an absurd figure that included, among other things, sauerkraut. Such ludicrous provisions created an image for national Prohibition that ran counterproductively to its effective enforcement.

Thus, with the crucial shift in philosophical support and with the absurdities of enforcement, Prohibition became marked by ineffective enforcement of and compliance with the law nationally. Nash has written that the rural areas continued to support Prohibition as "a way of expressing a preference for a stricter moral order and a cleaner, simpler nation such as existed in their memories of the past."[16] However, the increasing number of urbanites opposed Prohibition and avoided compliance with the law:

Spartan idealism was collapsing. People were tired of girding up their loins to serve noble causes. They were tired of making the United States a land fit for heroes to live in. They wanted to relax and be themselves. The change of feeling toward prohibition was bewilderingly rapid . . . the liquorless millennium had . . . been indefinitely postponed. [17]

With the change in attitude toward Prohibition came the concomitant exhibition of anti-Prohibition behavior. Despite the constant exhortations of the Anti-Saloon League, and despite the law enforcement efforts of the Prohibition Bureau, circumvention of the Eighteenth Amendment became the rule, rather than the exception. Home distilleries, imported alcohol, and illicit "speakeasies" became national symbols for a social policy that had lost the support of the American people. Violation of the law became so widespread that its effective enforcement became an impossibility. By 1925, it was estimated that only five percent of imported liquor and ten percent of illegal domestic alcohol were being captured annually by Prohibition agents.[18] Prohibition had become an unenforceable social policy.

Prohibitionists had claimed that the elimination of the alcoholic beverage traffic would produce massive societal rewards, such as the elimination of poverty, hunger, and economic woes. As the United States entered the Depression, it had become painfully clear that Prohibition could not live up to its promises. In recognition of this fact, the Twenty-First Amendment to the United States Constitution abrogated national Prohibition and brought an end to the "noble experiment."

Clarence Darrow's Position on Prohibition

Clarence Darrow enjoyed a national reputation for his opposition to Prohibition. This opposition is best understood as an extension of Darrow's general opposition to any manifestation of authority that tended to curtail any individual's rights and liberties. He believed that Prohibition was nothing more than another attempt to hamstring the freedom of expression and action that he dearly cherished. To Darrow, Prohibition was a symbol of the constant danger to individual freedom, a point illustrated in his autobiography:

. . . in prohibition I saw a grievous and far-reaching menace to the right of the individual. I knew it was supported by all the forces that were hostile to human freedom. I foresaw that it meant a fanaticism and intolerance that would hesitate at nothing to force its wishes and ways of life upon the world. [19]

Darrow saw Prohibition as but one part of a multifaceted threat to individual freedom.

Consistent with this fear, Darrow did not mince words in his constant denunciation of Prohibitionists and their cause. His characterization of the entire Prohibition movement was full of negatively-loaded labels:

. . . prohibitionists organized their forces and waged the campaign to destroy the liberties of American citizens. It was on this foundation that they foisted upon the United States a reign of terror, intimidation, violence, and bigotry unprecedented in the modern world. [20]

Prohibition, then, became the "devil term" in Darrow's concept of the national threat to human dignity and freedom.

It must be pointed out that Darrow did not come to this position of opposition against Prohibition in the 1920s; it developed much earlier than that. In 1909, some eleven years before the Eighteenth Amendment was added to the Constitution, Clarence Darrow first spoke out publicly against a policy of national prohibition. In a lecture before the New England United Labor League in New Bedford, Massachusetts, Darrow lashed out against Prohibitionists as the despoilers of individual freedom,[21] a position he maintained throughout the remainder of his life.

When Prohibition became part of the law of the land during the 1920s, Darrow continued his outspoken opposition to this social policy. He authored magazine articles on the subject,[22] presented many public lectures, and engaged in a number of debates that considered the philosophical and practical validity of Prohibition. Years later, Darrow asserted that this continual outpouring against Prohibition was necessitated by his own concept of human freedom: "I never missed a chance to speak or write against prohibition. It was a matter of fighting for the liberty of the individual."[23]

An interesting sidelight to this matter has been provided by Alan Hynd in *Defenders of the Damned*. One might expect that a man of Darrow's virulent opposition to Prohibition would utilize every opportunity to strike a blow against the hated law. In Darrow's case, this was not so. When he was given the chance to defend Chicago mobster Al Capone against alleged violations of the liquor law, Darrow responded to Capone's intermediary in the following manner:

Capone is helping to ruin this whole country with that stuff of his that is being sold to nice decent kids. You go back and tell that sonofabitch that there ain't enough money in the world for me to have anything to do with him. [24]

Instead of joining forces with unsavory underworld characters, Darrow chose to take to the public platform to debate Prohibition in an attempt to demonstrate its philosophical corruptness and its impracticality in application. Although records indicate that these public appearances were generally packed with anti-Prohibition audiences sympathetic to Darrow's views, his arguments reached untold thousands of people who had been either in favor of or uncommitted to this national policy.[25] This study concentrates upon two of these debates: Darrow vs. John Haynes Holmes in 1924 and Darrow vs. Wayne B. Wheeler in 1927.

Darrow vs. Holmes

Three weeks after the debate with Judge Talley on the issue of capital punishment, Clarence Darrow returned to New York City to debate John Haynes Holmes on the viability of Prohibition. Unlike Talley, Holmes generally shared a common philosophical agreement with Darrow, as he possessed a reputation as a defender of social justice. Holmes had been educated at Harvard, receiving his A.B. in 1902 and his S.T.B. in 1904. After ordination into the Unitarian ministry, Holmes became noteworthy for his ardent sermons that emphasized important social issues and for his outspoken pacifism and opposition to American involvement in the First World War. At the conclusion of that war, Holmes withdrew from the Unitarian ministry and established an independent organization, the Community Church of New York City, a nondenominational church that required no profession of faith.

By 1924, Reverend Holmes had established himself as a leading civil libertarian and was a director of the American Civil Liberties Union.[26]

With such a background, one might expect Holmes to have been in the ranks of the opposition to Prohibition; however, he was not. Instead, Holmes took the position that the Eighteenth Amendment was a positive good in its impact upon society. While he readily agreed that Prohibition curtailed the individual's liberties to some degree, his major concern was with the structure of society as a whole. Therefore, Holmes saw in Prohibition the chance to utilize the power of government to uplift society and to combat the many societal ills against which he had fought for so many years. The curtailment of one man's liberty, then, was justified if society as a whole would be improved. It was upon this point that Holmes's and Darrow's philosophies diverged.

Because these two national civil libertarians disagreed on the issue of Prohibition, the League for Political Discussion, a New York City-based organization, arranged a public debate that would allow the presentation of the divergent philosophies. The debate was staged at the Manhattan Opera House on December 14, 1924, before a very enthusiastic audience.[27] The League for Political Discussion hosted this debate because of that organization's concern with relevant political controversies. Benjamin A. Javits of the league explained that the central issue of the debate was personal liberty, an issue that transcended the prohibition of alcohol:

. . .*there is a great issue involved, which I am sure you will hear a great deal about, and that is whether the state, this nation, having a democratic form of government, has a right by legislation to regulate the private life of each person living under its flag.*

The issue is not confined to liquor alone. The Eighteenth Amendment indicates a trend on the part of governments, or on the part of government, through its legislatures, to take from individuals their liberty.[28]

The leaders of the League for Political Discussion saw Prohibition as something more than a mere restriction of the alcoholic beverage traffic.

Clarence Darrow was persuaded to return to New York City in mid-December of 1924 to debate Reverend Holmes on the following topic: "Resolved, that the United States should continue the policy of Prohibition as defined in the Eighteenth Amendment." As the chairman of the debate, the League for Political Discussion chose Royal S. Copeland, United States Senator from New York and an outspoken opponent of Prohibition. In his introduction of the issue of the debate, Senator Copeland attempted to demonstrate the significance of the forthcoming forensic struggle:

. . . *we are going to have a debate today on a subject which divides the American people. I doubt if any question since the abolition of slavery has so engrossed the thought of the American people as this question of prohibition . . . no matter where the subject of prohibition is concerned, whether it is in a Congress or in a church or on a street corner or in this great Opera House, you find assembling together a multitude of people, and every person present with some more or less fixed idea about the rights and wrongs of this great subject.*[29]

In recognition of the purported attitudes of the American people toward Prohibition, Senator Copeland's final remarks indicated that the purpose of the debate was informative, and not persuasive, in nature:

. . . the purpose of the debate is not to change opinion, but to make clear to both sides of this controversy that the men and women on each side of it are honest in their conviction. [30]

Despite Copeland's caveat, ballots were distributed to the members of the audience upon which the winner of the debate was to be recorded and returned to the League for Political Discussion by mail. No record exists of the results of this ballotting. [31]

Both Holmes and Darrow were allotted one hour of speaking time apiece in which to present their views and to refute the views of the opposition. As the affirmative spokesman in favor of the debate resolution, Reverend Holmes both began and concluded the confrontation.

Reverend Holmes's Argumentation and Strategy

As the affirmative speaker, John Haynes Holmes had the responsibility to provide reasons for the maintenance of the Eighteenth Amendment. Since this debate centered upon a question of public policy, it was incumbent upon Holmes to demonstrate both the need for and the practicality of Prohibition as defined and implemented by the constitutional provision. In upholding this burden, Holmes made it explicitly clear that his position was one of support for the Eighteenth Amendment and not for the Volstead Act:

. . . we are discussing the policy of prohibition from the standpoint of the Eighteenth Amendment to the Constitution, and not from the standpoint of the Volstead Act. I am ready to assume, from the very drop of the hat, that the Volstead Act is unwise and ineffective and is not a success. I shall simply decline to discuss at all the policy

of enforcement under the Volstead Act, but shall confine everything that I have to say this afternoon to the Eighteenth Amendment to the Constitution as a policy which should be continued by one form of legislation or another into the future. [32]

From the foregoing paragraph, it is obvious that Holmes went to some length to disassociate himself and his position from the Volstead Act, a move perceived by this writer as an overt bit of strategy on Holmes's part. It must be remembered that it was the Volstead Act that contained or encouraged the excesses in the implementation of Prohibition. It was the Volstead Act, not the Eighteenth Amendment, that outlawed certain types of sauerkraut and hair tonic. It was the utilization of the Volstead Act that created most of the problems for the public image of Prohibition. Therefore, by attempting to hammer a wedge between himself and this unpopular piece of legislation, Holmes tried to strengthen his argumentative position by dealing only with Prohibition in the theoretical sense in defending the vague Eighteenth Amendment. Thus, by narrowing the ground to be defended, Holmes attempted to maximize the possibility of persuading an audience that was, in general, overtly hostile to Prohibition. [33]

Despite this dichotomization, Darrow blended the Eighteenth Amendment and the Volstead Act together into one cohesive philosophical enemy. The reason for this action cannot be definitely known, but three possible explanations may be considered. First, it is possible that Darrow did not hear Holmes's disclaimer and was oblivious to the fact that Holmes refused to defend the Volstead Act. However, this does not seem likely, because Holmes took great pains in reiterating his disclaimer and it

46

occurred during the opening of his first presentation when other arguments had not yet been presented that might have confused matters. Second, it is possible that Darrow was committed to a prepared presentation and was, therefore, unable to modify his speech to take into account Holmes's disclaimer. Yet, George G. Whitehead, the director of Darrow's debate tours during the late 1920s and early 1930s has written that Darrow extemporized his debates and was not tied to a manuscript.[34] Apparently, Darrow spoke sparingly from notes throughout his debate career during this time. Therefore, only one other possibility remains: Darrow consciously avoided Holmes's disclaimer because of the desire to link the Volstead Act with the Eighteenth Amendment in order to improve the persuasive nature of his own line of argumentation. Darrow did not look upon these public debates as mere exercises of mental gymnastics; instead, he utilized these forums to propagate his views and to persuade others to his side of the issues:

I am inclined to think that everyone is a propagandist by nature. When one has an idea, he feels it his duty to share it with his fellow man. People want every one to believe as they believe, to see as they see. . . . And in this I have always been like the rest. I have sought to convert people. . . .[35]

Darrow's own words indicate that his goal in speaking was persuasion, and, in the debate with Holmes, his position was strengthened strategically by linking the Volstead Act with the Eighteenth Amendment. It is this writer's opinion that Darrow deliberately overlooked Holmes's disclaimer to improve his own strategic position while, at the same time, placing additional burden upon the argumentation to be offered by his opponent, an unethically effective stratagem.

In presenting the specifics of his affirmative case, Holmes adopted a strategy that is often suggested for dealing with an audience that is relatively hostile to one's position. Specifically, it is suggested that the speaker attempt to cause the audience to agree with many general statements so as to maximize the possibility of later agreement with more controversial statements.[36] Holmes implemented this strategic approach by arguing initially from general statements about the prohibition of many materials and leading to the specific justification of the Prohibition of the alcoholic beverage traffic (see Table II).

First, Holmes argued that the utilization of prohibitory legislation was not a new idea, but, on the contrary, a time-honored instrument of various democratic governments:

. . . prohibition is a policy which has had the support of democratic governments for I know not how many years in the past, and it is the policy which democratic societies have adopted everywhere for dealing with social questions of one kind or another.

It was a prohibition piece of legislation which England adopted for the abolition of the slave trade . . . . The League of Nations is adopting, or trying to adopt, the policy of prohibition in the matter of getting rid of opium and the opium traffic.

All these are prohibition measures. They are exactly the same kind of thing as we have embodied in the Eighteenth Amendment to the Constitution.[37]

The point of this argument was to demonstrate that Prohibition was not a radically new idea to limit the individual freedom of the American people. Instead, by suggesting a broad historical development of

Table II   Major Arguments in the Holmes-Darrow Debate

John Haynes Holmes	Clarence Darrow
Prohibition is a viable activity of democratic governments	Liberty cannot be entrusted to Prohibitionists —Prohibition is a symptom of intolerance —Liberty is being hedged in by fanatics
Prohibition is not a new social policy	
Prohibition differentiates between philosophical anarchism and philosophical socialism	This is a very hard line to find
Laws are necessary for the protection of society	Sixty percent of the people should not control the actions of others
There is a need to sacrifice the liberty of the individual for the safety of society	Prohibition is beyond reason and logic; some tolerance is needed
Prohibition is social legislation	We must be vigilant against the encroachment of rights by authorities
Liquor is dangerous to the public safety	It makes no sense to punish the nondrunkard —People who drink have contributed to society
Liquor allows the strong to exploit the weak	
Those opposed to Prohibition are selfish	
	Prohibition cannot be enforced
Prohibition can be repealed	Prohibition cannot be repealed

prohibitory legislation, Holmes attempted to build a chain of thought that would demonstrate that Prohibition was but another step in the beneficial social development of man. Holmes previewed this conclusion, or the final link of the chain, as he terminated this initial line of argumentation:

The Eighteenth Amendment came in the process of inevitable social development. It was the final fulfillment of a policy to which the overwhelming majority of the American people had long since dedicated themselves by the processes of democratic franchise and democratic legislation. [38]

From this point, Holmes then contended that laws were a necessary part of society to safeguard individual liberty in the general sense and the freedom and liberty of society as a whole. In recognition of this fact, Holmes then continued on to argue that there are instances when it was necessary to sacrifice individual liberty to secure the safety and liberty of the entire society:

. . . there are a whole lot of habits of individual life, things which individuals may do, which affect other people and therefore affect society, habits and standards which cannot be confined within the borders of the individual life but overflow and run out into the precincts of society. [39]

Therefore, according to Holmes,

"social legislation" was necessary to protect the whole of society from the actions of individual members of that society. In support of this position, he cited examples of traffic laws and sanitation codes to demonstrate that social legislation was a positive societal good. Thus, Holmes concluded that Prohibition was but another piece of social legislation that was designed to protect society from the excesses of individuals.[40]

Reverend Holmes utilized thirty minutes of his initial thirty-five minute presentation in developing the general lines of argumentation described over the past several pages. It was with but five minutes remaining that he quickly asserted two major harms resulting from the utilization of alcoholic beverages:

Liquor, in the first place, is dangerous to the public safety . . . . Liquor is dangerous to public safety because it creates poverty, it cultivates crime, it establishes social conditions generally which are a burden to society.

Secondly, liquor legislation is social legislation because liquor constitutes a deliberate exploitation of the weak by the strong. The real thing that the Eighteenth Amendment was after–the real thing–was the liquor business . . . a business in the hands of a few for the amassing of great millions which preyed upon the weaknesses of the people . . . .[41]

Because of these harms, Holmes concluded that Prohibition was a justifiable piece of social legislation that did *not* infringe upon the sanctity of personal liberty:

. . . I have never believed that democracy involved the liberty to guzzle when that liberty was a menace to me and to all other men and to the integrity of that society which constitutes the America we love together.[42]

Clarence Darrow's Argumentation and Strategy

As can be seen by a perusal of Reverend Holmes's line of argumentation, he opted for an affirmative case that was philosophically supportive of Prohibition. Only in the waning moments of his opening address did he consider specific indictments of alcohol and the consumption of alcoholic beverages. Darrow chose to utilize a different technique of argumentation. While he did offer philosophical objection to Holmes's position, he emphasized specific indictments of Prohibition as a social policy. Darrow's general attitude toward Prohibition, an attitude that was clearly expressed in the debate with Holmes, was delineated in his autobiography:

I advocate the fullest liberty of self-expression, and long before prohibition became the policy of the United States I had fought for the right of the individual to choose his own life. By that I mean, doing the things he wants to do.[43]

In the presentation of this counter-philosophical argument, Darrow took exception to Holmes's position that prohibitive legislation was a viable activity of democratic governments. On the contrary, he claimed that prohibitive legislation was antithetical to liberty, and this argument was presented by way of humorous example:

I say that nobody in their right senses would trust their individual liberty to the people who believe in that sort of legislation.

My friend says he believes in liberty–liberty of speech, liberty of the press. Yet, I can talk about beer, but I can't drink it. What is the use of talking about it? All that makes it worse when I can't drink it. Right now in this discussion I get thirsty just talking about it. Can you have any liberty without liberty of action? [44]

Extending this line of argumentation, Darrow claimed that so-called social legislation, such as Prohibition, was really an expression of intolerance toward another's way of life, and he questionably analogized Prohibition with witch-burning in New England during the seventeenth century. [45] He concluded that "almost every sort of conduct has been hedged around in this world of fanatics," implicitly referring to 1920s Prohibitionists.

In response to Holmes's argument that laws were necessary for the preservation of society and that, sometimes, individual liberty had to be sacrificed for the safety of society, Darrow charged that the allowance of sixty percent of the populace to create criminal statutes would eventually mean the loss of personal liberty within the United States. Sounding very much like John Stuart Mill, he spoke of his fear of tyranny established by the ruling majority:

If the doctrine should prevail that when sixty percent of the people of a country believe that certain conduct should be a criminal offense and for that conduct they must send the forty percent to jail, then liberty is dead and freedom is gone. They will first destroy the forty percent and then turn and destroy each other. [46]

It was within this argument that Darrow called for increased tolerance of others' ways of life, religious convictions, and customs. For Darrow, Prohibition was but the tip of the iceberg of societal intolerance, and he feared that the Eighteenth Amendment might be utilized as a precedent for later prohibitive legislation that would circumscribe individual liberty to an even greater degree.

The strength of this argument lay not only in the sincere advocacy by which it was presented by Darrow but also in the spectre of future infringement upon personal liberty that the argument probably created for the members of the audience. Reverend Holmes must have believed this argument to have been somewhat compelling, because it was one of but three arguments to which he offered any serious rebuttal. As might be expected, Holmes claimed that if the people did not like Prohibition, then they could certainly repeal the Eighteenth Amendment. [47] In refutation of Holmes's response, Darrow utilized some statistical analysis to argue that the repeal of Prohibition was impossible:

I don't know whether Doctor Holmes knows that out of 110,000,000 people in the United States, 6,000,000 mainly located in the Prohibition States–6,000,000 people out of 110,000,000 can prevent the repeal of the Eighteenth Amendment. We have no democracy when it comes to that–and never did have. I don't care if three-quarters of the people in the United States vote for repeal–you can't get rid of it that way. [48]

The tide of events, of course, would prove Darrow wrong. Prohibition was repealed almost nine years to the day of the Holmes-Darrow debate.

In response to the two specific indictments against alcohol brought by Holmes, Darrow responded with point-by-point refutation. First, in answer to the charge that Prohibition was necessary to protect the general public, Darrow claimed that it made no sense to penalize the nondrunkard. All of Holmes's examples of the barbarous influences of alcohol were drawn from individuals who consumed alcohol to excess—the drunken driver and the drunken working man. Darrow charged that Prohibition was nonsensical because it penalized the nonexcessive drinker as well as the drunkard:

. . . if I want to take a drink and do not get drunk where I interfere with anybody else, should society then tell me that I can't drink . . . is that any reason why I, who do not get drunk, shall not have anything to drink? [49]

The strategy underlying this argument was the creation of an appearance of sanity and reason on the part of the anti-Prohibitionists to contrast with the irrationality of the Prohibitionists. To implement this strategy, Darrow utilized the tactic of simplification: make a complex issue appear simple so that the divergent positions are quite clear to the audience. By suggesting that the Eighteenth Amendment discriminated irrationally against the nonexcessive alcoholic consumer, Darrow was able to create the impression that Prohibition was wholesale intolerance.

Second, in response to the argument that alcohol allowed the strong to exploit the weak, Darrow attempted to create the counterimpression that the consumer of alcohol was no weakling but was, on the contrary, a crucial element to the society. To do this, Darrow argued that "wets" have contributed greatly to society, again couching his argument in humorous style:

Take out of this world the men who have drunk, down through the past, and you would take away all the poetry and literature and practically all the works of genius that the world has produced. What kind of a poem do you suppose you would get out of a glass of ice-water? [50]

Thus, consumers of alcohol were not continually the downtrodden of society; instead, they were members of the most productive element of that society. This argument probably had great impact upon the majority of the debate audience—they were members of the great productive "wet" elite.

Finally, Darrow lodged an argument of impracticality against the implementation and enforcement of Prohibition. The Eighteenth Amendment had not eliminated drinking; it had not dried up the nation. According to Darrow, Prohibition had been a dismal failure:

I never knew anybody with money who couldn't get a drink. Do any of you? . . . I never knew anybody in this land of ours, under the Amendment and under the Volstead Act, to go thirsty.

Of course, it has raised the price . . . . It has substituted whiskey for beer to many people–which I think is a poor substitution. [51]

The implicit meaning underlying this argument was that if something did not work, then it should be abandoned. If Prohibition failed to achieve its goals, then Prohibition should be abandoned as a national policy. It was with this argument that Darrow linked the Volstead Act with the Eighteenth Amendment, over Holmes's disclaimer, and argued that its impracticality necessitated its repeal.

Darrow vs. Holmes: Evaluation

As was the case with most of Darrow's public debates, the various rebuttal periods within the Holmes-Darrow debate did little to clarify or expand the issues developed in the initial presentations by both debaters. In general, the rebuttal periods found a mere repetition of earlier arguments and refutation, a point that was especially accurate for Holmes's later speeches. Both debaters tended to drop their major lines of argumentation in favor of concentrating upon the major philosophical difference that existed between them: the plea for social legislation versus the plea for tolerance in human interaction.

The debaters afforded an interesting contrast in both style and manner of speaking. Reverend Holmes presented his position in a straightforward manner that was directly to the point. Each one of his arguments was designed to mesh well with the philosophical supportive case for Prohibition that he attempted to construct. The organization of the material was clear; the specific arguments with the substructure flowed well. Darrow, on the other hand, utilized a rambling style of organization that skipped hurriedly from one argument to another. Although major ideas were developed in detail, their development took place throughout several varied parts of his initial presentation, creating a choppiness within his dispositional framework. Instead of proceeding along the lines of argumentative organization as laid out by Holmes, Darrow chose to offer refutation within an arbitrary arrangement of arguments. This seeming shortcoming or disadvantage was offset by the significant utilization of humor to create a favorable audience attitude toward his position. This one factor demonstrated the largest divergence of style: Darrow utilized a great amount of humor to support his arguments and to deprecate those of his opposition, while Holmes utilized humor minimally.

As to the argumentative positions of the debaters, this writer has discerned shortcomings on the part of both Holmes and Darrow. First, as the spokesman for the affirmative, it was Holmes's responsibility to crystallize major arguments on behalf of the policy of Prohibition, reasons as to why such a national policy was

a societal necessity. Instead of doing this, Holmes spent the vast majority of his speaking time defending prohibitive legislation in general; only the final five minutes dealt with Prohibition itself. It is quite possible to accept ninety per cent of Holmes's position and still be able to condemn the Eighteenth Amendment. In short, while the history of prohibitive legislation was quite interesting, its overall value to the topic for debate was, at best, minimal.

Second, when Holmes did present two hurriedly developed specific indictments against alcohol, he failed to respond to Darrow's objections to these points. If Prohibition is to be justified because of the evils of alcohol, then it is incumbent upon the affirmative speaker to crystallize, support, and then resupport the reality of these evils. Reverend Holmes failed to uphold this burden. Instead, he chose to defend Prohibition on a philosophical plane, a strategic choice that tended to weaken his overall argumentative position.

Clarence Darrow, as the negative spokesman, had the responsibility of responding to Holmes's arguments and developing arguments against the Eighteenth Amendment. In the first case, he did respond to every major argument offered by Holmes, but there were instances when his responses were not as adequate as they should have been. For example, Darrow's argument that "wets" have contributed to the functioning of society had little to do with Holmes's argument that alcohol allowed the strong to exploit the weak. The emphasis of the affirmative indictment was that the liquor industry manipulated the poor working man of society. Darrow's argument, while relatively sound in itself, did not actually come to grips with the thrust of Holmes's indictment. Here was a clash of arguments that was, in reality, no clash at all.

As far as Darrow's charges against Prohibition were concerned, he certainly could have expanded his claim that it was impossible to enforce. Instead of driving home this charge of impracticality, Darrow inferred his argument more than he crystallized it. Holmes attempted to draw a dichotomy between the Eighteenth Amendment and the Volstead Act; Darrow would have been justified in denying this strategic ploy. After all, without the enforcing power of the Volstead Act, the Eighteenth Amendment was virtually meaningless. Therefore, Darrow could have strengthened his position by overtly rejecting Holmes's dichotomy and forcing the affirmative speaker to defend the totality of Prohibition. Such a move would have allowed Darrow to pursue his indictment of impracticality more fully and would have improved his pragmatic indictments of Prohibition. However, despite the fact that the argument Darrow did utilize was relatively weak, Holmes did not attempt to offer any refutation to this point.

In a final piece of evaluation, this writer would assert that Darrow carried the majority of the arguments tendered within the debate and that his position was immeasurably aided by the weak philosophical case offered by Holmes. Although the affirmative speaker had the possibilities of a strong position, the generalized line of argumentation, plus the failure to respond to the majority of the negative indictments, caused the negative to gain the strategic upper hand—an advantage maintained by Darrow throughout the debate. Darrow's indictments carried the debate; this writer would vote for the negative. Unfortunately, the results of the audience vote were never publicized.

Darrow vs. Wheeler

Because Clarence Darrow considered Prohibition to be symptomatic of a national stream of intolerance and the beginning point of increased governmental infringement upon personal liberty, he never avoided an opportunity to debate the merits of this national policy before public forums. Thus, between 1924 and 1929, Darrow debated the policy of Prohibition more than any other topic before gatherings of individuals across the United States.

One gentleman who twice clashed with Darrow over Prohibition was Wayne Bidwell Wheeler of the Anti-Saloon League. Darrow and Wheeler met in a radio debate in Chicago in March of 1926 and, for the second time, at New York City's Carnegie Hall in April of 1927.[52] It is with this second debate that the present study is concerned.

Wayne B. Wheeler spent the entirety of his adult life in the employ of the Anti-Saloon League, having joined that organization in 1894 upon graduation from Oberlin College. Because of his sincere zeal and tireless efforts on behalf of the league, Wheeler moved very quickly into the organization's hierarchy, becoming its general counsel in 1917 and the legislative superintendent of the Anti-Saloon League in 1919. Because of these positions, Wheeler took part in aiding state prohibition leagues in the creation of anti-alcohol laws. So active was Wheeler that "he wrote or aided in framing local option and prohibition laws for nearly all the states."[53]

Because of his monumental efforts on behalf of the Anti-Saloon League, Wheeler became, by the early 1920s, the national symbol of the league itself, a fact illustrated by Justin Steuart, Wheeler's publicity secretary:

The Anti-Saloon League of America is a dream made flesh and blood by Howard Hyde Russell. It became the mightiest political force in the nation through the statesmanlike vision of Purley A. Baker. It propagandized two generations through the sagacity of its philosopher, Ernest H. Cherrington. It won its greatest legislative victories through its legislative superintendent, Edwin C. Dinwiddie. It was directed by a group of the sanest minds in the nation. But in the thought of the American people, the Anti-Saloon League was Wayne B. Wheeler, its victories were all won by Wayne B. Wheeler, and it died with Wayne B. Wheeler. [54]

Therefore, pitting Darrow against Wheeler in a debate on Prohibition was a "natural": Darrow was the leading anti-Prohibitionist of the public lecture circuit, while Wheeler was the public symbol of the entire Prohibition movement.

Because of the importance of Prohibition politically, many organizations sponsored public debates on this issue after 1926. It was seen by many persons that the presidential election of 1928 would probably match a "wet" against a "dry" in a national referendum upon the desirability of Prohibition. To take advantage of this fact, groups across the United States hosted Prohibition debates between major political, social, and educational leaders. In keeping with this trend, the American Forum, another New York City-based political discussion organization, decided to bring Darrow and Wheeler together for the biggest Prohibition debate of them all. On April 10, 1927, Ernest J. Howe, president of the American Forum, announced that special invitations to attend the debate had been sent to the major Democratic and Republican presidential possibilities. Howe also announced that the purpose of this debate was

"to afford any potential presidential candidate an excellent opportunity to hear both sides of the question expounded by two remarkable men." [55] In keeping with such a monumental forensic clash, Carnegie Hall was secured as the scene for the debate, and Mayor James Walker of New York City was persuaded to serve as the debate's presiding officer.

Wheeler was apparently pleased with the forthcoming second encounter with Darrow, because, speaking from his Washington office on April 19, he said:

I like to debate with such a man because he shows his own crowd how some of their arguments look. Mr. Darrow is a good example of individualism going the limit and self-determination that is indifferent to the public welfare.

We will fight it out at Carnegie Hall in New York next Saturday night without gloves. The rules of the bloodless battle will be catch-as-catch-can. [56]

Such fiery statements were doubtless pleasing to the American Forum, whose leaders constantly ballyhooed the upcoming debate as the confrontation of the decade. Since the price of admission was fairly inexpensive, tickets costing between $1.65 and $3.30, the Forum leaders thought that Carnegie Hall might not be able to hold the would-be audience, and contingency plans were made to shift the debate to a larger meeting hall if the overflow became too great.

On the evening of the debate, April 23, 1927, all of the forum's assumptions and loftiest dreams collapsed. Eight special police had been hired as security officers to prevent the rival "wet" and "dry" factions from clawing at each other's throats; no incident occurred. Only one person was ejected from the debate, and that was for "distributing handbills advertising the sale of grape juice which time and nature would turn into wine."[57] The expectations of an overflow crowd never materialized as but 2,500 people showed up for the debate; Carnegie Hall had a seating capacity in excess of 3,000. The debate itself began late because of the twenty-minute tardiness of Mayor Walker, Wheeler was so ill with a lung infection that his opening speech had to be read for him, and the "wets" so controlled the audience that they "kept up an almost continuous series of heckling and interruptions during the time Mr. Wheeler had the floor."[58] In short, the debate that took place was not the debate planned by the American Forum. Gate receipts were barely able to meet the evening's expenses of over $3,000.

Clarence Darrow's Argumentation and Strategy

Because of the negatively-phrased wording of the debate topic, "Resolved: that the prohibition of the beverage liquor traffic is detrimental to the public welfare," Clarence Darrow served as the affirmative spokesman in the debate with Wheeler. Unlike the debate with Reverend Holmes, this debate topic centered upon a proposition of value, not a proposition of policy. This is a crucial distinction, because propositions of value allow the debater greater freedom in the quality of arguments to be covered. Since the topic contained an inherent appeal to the latent biases and prejudices of the audience members, the debaters did not have to develop arguments in as much detail as was necessary under a proposition of policy.

In identifying and analyzing Darrow's major lines of

argumentation, there is a great similarity between the arguments offered in the Holmes and Wheeler debates (see Table III). As in the debate with Holmes, Darrow emphasized the importance of man's having individual freedom to choose his own lifestyle and to do what he wished:

Instead of setting everybody to govern everybody else, each man ought to have something to do with the job of controlling himself. And if he has any liberty whatever it seems to me he ought to have a right to say what he should eat and what he should drink!

. . . any degree of individual freedom should leave a man free to choose. [59]

Darrow extended this argument, again, to include Prohibitionists in the same class with those who executed women in New England for witchcraft, thereby attempting to color the audience's conception of the proponents of the Prohibition movement. Since this debate was one of value judgment, a debater could enjoy an immense strategic advantage by placing his opposition in an unfavorable light. Darrow sought this advantage by creating the impression that Prohibitionists were crazed fanatics, men who constantly attempted to circumscribe unnaturally the liberties of men who disagreed with their position.[60]

After lodging this philosophical indictment against Prohibition, Darrow began a series of pragmatic indictments against this national policy. First, Darrow claimed that Prohibition was a detrimental policy because it was ineffective in drying up America:

Personally I have never yet noticed any drought. And I never expect to. All that has been accomplished is to take beer and wine away from people who can't afford the high prices. That is all. But they are

Table III   Major Arguments in the Darrow-Wheeler Debate

Clarence Darrow	Wayne Wheeler
Man should have individual freedom	Public welfare should come first in determining policies
Prohibition is ineffective	
Prohibition cannot be enforced	Not concerned with enforcement
The Volstead Act is impractical	
People will only obey those laws they believe in	People must obey the law
Alcohol does not cause all of society's problems	Alcohol is harmful to its users —People have the right to better their condition —Alcohol has no inherent right to exist
The majority of the people oppose Prohibition	The majority of the people support Prohibition

getting around that. They are buying grape juice and letting the Lord make the wine for them. [61]

Although he never finally closed this line of argumentation, Darrow's probable intent in laying out this objection was to justify the elimination of the Eighteenth Amendment and the Volstead Act altogether. If Prohibition failed to meet its goal, it might be argued, then there was no longer a viable rationale for the continuance of an ineffective public policy. Here was an argument of utility: if it does not work, throw it out.

Second, extending his initial analysis that man ought to have the fullest extent of possible individual liberty, Darrow argued a second utilization concept, that Prohibition could not be enforced:

It has never been enforced. It can never be enforced! Until the last spark of independence has fled from the heart of the American people they will never consent that an organized body of men shall tell them what they may drink and

what they may not drink . . . . There are jurors today who have too much manhood to sit upon a jury and convict a fellow man for doing exactly what he has done and is doing! . . . Juries refuse to convict for doing what they have done, and there are even judges who refuse to fine and imprison for doing what they habitually do! [62]

Again, the strategic point of this line of argumentation was to propose that a policy which would not, or could not, be enforced was not a viable public policy and should be abrogated.

Third, Darrow argued that Prohibition was a perversion of the United States Constitution in that it was antithetical to the expressed purposes of the Constitution itself. In Darrow's mind, the Constitution was written to provide safeguards for individual liberty against the encroachments of the ruling majority; Prohibition institutionalized such an encroachment upon liberty:

They ought to be proud of their work. These [prohibitionist] people do not even believe in a rule by majority. They have taken the Constitution of the United States, which so far as any legislation of this sort is concerned is meant simply for the protection of individual liberty against the majority, for there are some things that even majorities ought not to be able to do . . . . [63]

Thus, Darrow denied the legalistic underpinning supporting the Eighteenth Amendment. Despite the fact that Prohibition had been ruled constitutional, Darrow claimed that its provisions were contrary to the rationale for the existence of the Constitution. Such an argument depended entirely upon the value in the Constitution held by the various members of the audience.

Finally, Darrow's last line of argumentation returned to the idea of practicality, containing three separate arguments that denied the practical feasibility of Prohibition. He maintained that there had been a shift in public opinion over the past few years so that, by 1927, the majority of the American people were opposed to Prohibition. [64] This assertion served as the core of this final structure of argumentation, because it was from this point that Darrow claimed that people will obey those laws in which they have some measure of faith and belief: "people believe in enforcing only those laws that they believe in." [65] Therefore, since people must believe in those laws that may be effectively enforced, and since the majority of the people no longer had faith in the rationale for Prohibition, Darrow concluded that Prohibition was an impractical statute that was detrimental to the expressed public welfare and should be abrogated.

Basically, then, Darrow followed a line of argumentation that emphasized the impracticality of Prohibition, an impracticality that thwarted the desires of the majority of the people. Since he was utilitarian in nature, Darrow asserted that this impractical measure necessitated immediate remedy—the elimination of Prohibition through the abrogation of the Eighteenth Amendment and the Volstead Act. One is able to see that this emphasis upon utility is a different strategy than that of philosophical liberty as maintained during the debate with Reverend Holmes, but the final point was the same: Prohibition must go!

Wayne Wheeler's Argumentation and Strategy

Because Wayne Wheeler was ill, he elected to have his first presentation read from manuscript by F. Scott McBride, the national superintendent of the Anti-Saloon League. [66] As might be expected from a presentation of a prepared manuscript, most of Wheeler's initial presentation was concerned more with the construction of a pro-Prohibition case than with refutation of Darrow's line of argumentation. Refutation of the affirmative position, an inherent responsibility of any negative speaker, was offered by Wheeler himself during the rebuttal period. To facilitate the understanding of the major arguments involved, Wheeler's lines of argumentation throughout the constructive and rebuttal periods have been conjoined to allow a meaningful juxtaposition with Darrow's lines of argumentation.

In considering Darrow's philosophical position that man should be granted great degrees of personal freedom and liberty, Wheeler responded that the primary factor to be weighed must be the common good of society:

In determining what should be our course in framing the legislative policy of the nation, the public welfare should come before individual desires or selfish purposes. [67]

Herein, this argument is virtually the same as the philosophical argument upon which Reverend Holmes based his support of Prohibition. In short, the constant battle of individual liberty vs. the protection of society surfaced again during the Darrow-Wheeler debate. However, this did not serve as the major focal point of contention and attention as it had during the Holmes-Darrow confrontation.

It was at this point that Wheeler issued a caveat that was designed to eliminate the vast majority of Darrow's indictments against Prohibition: he refused to deal with arguments that concerned themselves with the practical enforcement of the national policy, stating simply that he would "set aside the controversy as to its enforcement."[68] From a strategic standpoint, one is able to perceive one advantage and one disadvantage in taking such a position. First, that caveat is advantageous because it eliminates the consideration of the major portion of Darrow's indictments. By doing so, Wheeler did not have to refute the arguments that Prohibition was ineffective, that the Volstead Act was impractical, and that Prohibition could never be enforced. In that respect, Wheeler's refusal to deal with the practical aspects of Prohibition could be construed as advantageous. However, in its final impact upon the debate, Wheeler's position most certainly was disadvantageous.

By leaving the area of the practicality of Prohibition entirely to Darrow, Wheeler virtually conceded the fact that Prohibition was a viable policy in theory only, that it could not be effectively implemented. All of Darrow's objections to the functioning workability of the Eighteenth Amendment and the Volstead Act remained unanswered and unrefuted, a sufficient reason unto itself for a person to adopt Darrow's position. Wheeler's caveat was, at best, a strategic blunder in open debate. He might have been able to salvage this point had he provided some rationale, some sort of justification for this position, but he did not do so. Instead, he merely stated that he was not going to concern himself with the practicalities of enforcement and moved on to another point. Considering the debate as a whole, this was a massive forensic error.

Having abandoned consideration of the enforcement of Prohibition, Wheeler proceeded to combine two of Darrow's arguments and to offer refutation to them. Darrow had argued that Prohibition was a perversion of the United States Constitution and that the American people would obey only those laws in which they had faith and belief. Wheeler responded that the people could amend the Constitution to do away with Prohibition, but, until that time, they had the responsibility to obey the law:

. . . those who are opposed to any part of the Constitution or the laws of the land have the right to join with others to bring about their amendment or repeal, but that until they are legally changed or repealed they should be obeyed and enforced. [69]

Darrow's response to this argument was the same as that offered to Reverend Holmes, that a small minority of individuals could thwart the repeal of the Eighteenth Amendment:

. . . the people who believe in that accursed legislation have one thing and one thing only to rely on, and that is they can find 6,000,000 people to prevent the repeal of the Constitution and can cajole

the people of the United States into the
idea that they must have prohibition.
That is what they are up against today. [70]

This argument was carried throughout the debate, but was mainly repeated by both debaters with a minimum of extension based upon the opposition's line of argumentation.

Finally, after listing the evil consequences stemming from the consumption of alcoholic beverages, Wheeler claimed that, in recognition of such evils, the vast majority of the American people continued to support Prohibition, thereby denying Darrow's final line of argumentation. To substantiate this claim, Wheeler adopted an historical approach to demonstrate that the people had wanted Prohibition for a number of years:

With the rising tide of sentiment against
intoxicating liquor, the appeal was made
in the name of democracy to allow the
majority of the people to determine
whether or not they wanted the beverage
liquor traffic in that community . . . .

The more the people discussed the
question the more convinced they became
that the beverage liquor traffic was a
menace to public health and safety . . . so
that twenty-five states were dry by a vote
of the people before national prohibition.

. . . we find that 95 per cent of the
territory of the nation was dry before
national prohibition and that 68 per cent
of the people lived in that territory. [71]

Based on this development, Wheeler argued that the people still wanted to continue Prohibition, utilizing this historical narrative as *prima facie* substantiation for his claim. Here, too, was another argument that repeatedly occurred throughout the debate but whose impact was minimized by its failure to deal with the specifics of the affirmative indictment.

Darrow vs. Wheeler: Evaluation

As has been suggested in the description of Wayne Wheeler's lines of argumentation, his decision to avoid consideration of the Darrow indictments against the impracticalities of the implementation of Prohibition was a damaging bit of strategy. Had Wheeler attempted to justify this move, it might have made his unresponsiveness more palatable, but he offered no sort of justification or rationalization. Thus, he handed Darrow the strategic advantage of being able to attack the impracticalities of Prohibition with no fear of negative refutation. Darrow converted this advantage into a devastating broadside against a policy which was shown to be viable only in a theoretical sense. Most policy concepts appear sound theoretically, but the real test of their utility comes from the experiences gained by their implementation. Wheeler granted a *de facto* admission to Darrow that Prohibition was not a functioning efficient policy, thereby allowing Darrow to secure concurrence with his position. Because of this factor alone, Clarence Darrow should be given the decision in the debate with Wayne Wheeler.

Several other remarks concerning the remainder of the lines of argumentation found within this debate are relevant. First, the perennial struggle between individual freedom and the necessity of protecting society fell within the large arena called personal value judgment. If the audience member were predisposed towards a relatively libertarian view of life, then he would have agreed with Darrow; if he were not he would have sided with Wheeler. This is the sort of argument that is well-tailored for the type of value proposition utilized within this debate.

Second, whether or not Prohibition could be or should be enforced depended upon the individual's conceptualization of law and society. A person who adhered to a strict legalistic interpretation of the statute books would be inclined to agree with Wheeler that "everyone should obey the law." Another individual with a utilitarian concept of the law would agree with Darrow that "if it does not work, get rid of it." So, again, we have another argument that would stand up well in a debate on a topic of value, but would not stand so well in a policy debate.

Third, the conflicting arguments as to whether or not the American people continued to support Prohibition allowed the audience member to reach no definite conclusion. This was unfortunate because this was the only argument which was factual in nature that drew contentions from both of the debaters. Darrow's claim that the people opposed Prohibition was based only upon blatant, unsupported assertion. Wheeler's claim that the people continued to support Prohibition was based upon antiquated recitations of history that did not deal with the specific Darrow argument that there had been a shift in public opinion. This writer would conclude that the audience probably accepted Darrow's argument, because it was during this time that it was estimated that Prohibition had had little effect upon the drinking habits of Americans. In all probability, a large portion of the debate audience frequented gin parlors and speakeasies, thereby providing living testimony to Darrow's claim.

Although no formal decision was rendered, the overt audience responses transcribed during the debate indicated that the audience tended to side with Darrow's position more than with Wheeler's. The *New York Times*, in reporting the debate, chronicled the audience reaction:

There was no decision but Mr. Darrow plainly had the sympathies of the audience, which gave him long and repeated cheers and applause, while it mingled boos, catcalls, jeers, hisses, and other derisive noises with the applause Mr. Wheeler received. [72]

When Darrow had debated Wheeler in 1926 over the radio, listeners were asked to vote for their favorite by telephone. Darrow won that balloting by a margin of nine to one. When one considers the specifics of the argumentative substructure and the overt audience responses, it can be concluded that Clarence Darrow also won the debate at Carnegie Hall in 1927.

Footnotes

1 Eighteenth Amendment to the Constitution of the United States of America.

2 James H. Timberlake, *Prohibition and the Progressive Movement, 1900-1920* (Cambridge, 1963), pp. 39-40.

3 Andrew Sinclair, *Prohibition: The Era of Excess* (Boston, 1962), p. 4.

4 Timberlake, p. 100.

5 *Ibid.*, p. 2.

6 Paul A. Carter, *The Decline and Revival of the Social Gospel: Social and Political Liberalism in American Protestant Churches, 1920-1940* (Ithaca, 1954), p. 5.

7 Timberlake, p. 66.

8 Carter, p. 33.

9 Don S. Kirschner, *City and Country–Rural Responses to Urbanization in the 1920s* (Westport, 1970), p. 26.

10 *Ibid.*, pp. 130-131.

11 Sinclair, pp. 23-24.

12 Frederick Lewis Allen, *Only Yesterday* (New York, 1931), p. 175.

13 The rhetorical importance of "devil terminology" is carefully explored by Richard Weaver, *The Ethics of Rhetoric* (Chicago, 1953), pp. 219-224.

14 Sinclair, pp. 400-401.

15 Carter, p. 38.

16 Roderick Nash, *The Nervous Generation: American Thought, 1917-1930* (Chicago, 1970), p. 145.

17 Allen, p. 177.

18 Dumas Malone and Basil Rauch, *War and Troubled Peace, 1917-1939* (New York, 1960), p. 151.

19 Clarence Darrow, *The Story of My Life* (New York, 1932), pp. 284-285.

20 *Ibid.*, pp. 290-291.

21 Abe C. Ravitz, *Clarence Darrow and the American Literary Tradition* (Cleveland, 1962), p. 127. This initial opposition to Prohibition is also confirmed by Irving Stone, *Clarence Darrow for the Defense* (Garden City, 1941), p. 487.

22 See, for example, Clarence Darrow, "The Ordeal of Prohibition," *The American Mercury*, II (August, 1924), pp. 419-427.

23 Darrow, *The Story of My Life*, p. 301.

24 Alan Hynd, *Defenders of the Damned* (New York, 1960), p. 117.

25 Ravitz, pp. 129-130.

26 *The National Cyclopedia of American Biography*, 1930, C, pp. 461-462.

27 The *New York Times*, December 15, 1924, p. 13.

28 Clarence Darrow and John Haynes Holmes, *Debate on Prohibition* (Girard, 1924), p. 5.

29 *Ibid.*, p. 7.

30 *Ibid.*, p. 8.

31 The *New York Times*, December 15, 1924, p. 13.

32 Darrow and Holmes, pp. 11-12.

33 The transcript of the Holmes-Darrow debate contains the overt audience reactions of applause and laughter. These reactions tend to indicate that the audience was decidedly "wet" in temperament.

34 George G. Whitehead, *Clarence Darrow–The Big Minority Man* (Girard, 1929), p. 6.

35 Darrow, *The Story of My Life*, p. 282.

36 Many basic speech texts advocate this method for dealing with "hostile" audiences. See, for example, Alan H. Monroe, *Principles and Types of Speech*, fifth edition (Chicago, 1962), p. 161; and Glenn R. Capp, *Basic Oral Communication* (Englewood Cliffs, 1971), pp. 70-71.

37 Darrow and Holmes, p. 12.

38 *Ibid.*, p. 15.

39 *Ibid.*, p. 22.

40 *Ibid.*, p. 25.

41 *Ibid.*, p. 26.

42 *Ibid.*, p. 27.

43 Darrow, *The Story of My Life*, p. 284.

44 Darrow and Holmes, p. 32.

45 *Ibid.*, p. 38.

46 *Ibid.*, p. 40.

[47] *Ibid.*, p. 49.

[48] *Ibid.*, p. 50.

[49] *Ibid.*, p. 31.

[50] *Ibid.*, p. 37.

[51] *Ibid.*, p. 34.

[52] The *New York Times*, April 9, 1927, p. 1.

[53] *The National Cyclopedia of American Biography*, 1927, B, p. 14.

[54] Justin Steuart, *Wayne Wheeler: Dry Boss* (New York, 1938), pp. 11-12.

[55] The *New York Times*, April 11, 1927, p. 14.

[56] The *New York Times*, April 20, 1927, p. 13.

[57] The *New York Times*, April 24, 1927, p. 1.

[58] *Ibid.*

[59] Clarence Darrow and Wayne B. Wheeler, *Dry-Law Debate* (Girard, 1927), p. 4.

[60] Darrow often referred to Prohibitionists as "fanatics," including Wheeler within this term of opprobrium. See Darrow, *The Story of My Life*, p. 292.

[61] Darrow and Wheeler, p. 7.

[62] *Ibid.*, pp. 9-10.

[63] *Ibid.*, p. 7.

[64] *Ibid.*, p. 32.

[65] *Ibid.*, p. 22.

[66] In reporting the Darrow-Wheeler debate, the *New York Times* inaccurately assigned Mr. McBride the initial of "C.," referring to him as C. Scott McBride. See the *New York Times*, April 24, 1927, p. 28.

[67] Darrow and Wheeler, p. 11.

[68] *Ibid.*

[69] *Ibid.*, p. 10.

[70] *Ibid.*, p. 32.

[71] *Ibid.*, pp. 16-17.

[72] The *New York Times*, April 24, 1927, p. 1.

Chapter Five

Man and God and Life

The decade of the 1920s witnessed many sets of conflicts within American society that both sprang from and added to a general feeling of societal dissonance. While these various conflicts centered upon differing issues of concern, all took place within the same historical setting that had been molded by the aftermath of the First World War, the tensions of an increasingly mobile society, and the factors of urbanization and industrialization. The United States was a scene of general "commotion, turbulence, and flux" during the third decade of the twentieth century.[1]

Within this scene of dissonance and uncertainty there arose the growth of a movement known as the fundamentalist movement in American religion, wherein a strict interpretation of the Biblical scriptures and a literal faith in the Bible's instructions came to the fore in many religious sects. One purpose of this movement was the provision of societal stability, a factor noted by Allan Sager:

. . .the psychological climate of the twenties was one in which men were made to feel that the foundations beneath them were tottering, if indeed not crumbling. Fundamentalists sensed that the supreme task before them was the buttressing of the old foundations and that certainly the future of Christianity–if not of humanity–depended upon the spirit and thoroughness with which they accomplished that task.[2]

The fundamentalist movement might best be seen and understood in contrast with the religious Social Gospel movement that had been initiated during the latter quarter of the nineteenth century. Specifically, whereas the Social Gospel emphasized the concept that "religious judgment is to be passed . . . upon the collective institutions which men have made" and called for direct social action to combat society's ills,[3] the fundamentalist movement emphasized the importance of the individual in salvation and redemption, thereby denying the societal milieu of the Social Gospel. Thus, while the Social Gospel exhorted its adherents to take part in rectifying the problems plaguing American society because of one's duty to God through his fellow men, the fundamentalist movement presented an antithetical philosophy that instructed its adherents to work to salvage one's own individual soul.

In addition, whereas many of those within the camp of the Social Gospel accepted many of the findings of recent laboratory and social science scholarship and internalized them into a program of action, the fundamentalist movement tended to exhibit a defensive response to such matters.[4] Fundamentalists felt that the use of such information and knowledge revealed by recent research was worthless. If this material did damage to the sanctity of Biblical scriptures, then it might also lead the people away from the only true means by which society could be saved—the Second Coming of Christ.[5] Thus, the Social Gospel movement and the fundamentalist movement differed significantly over the purpose of the existence of religion and over its duties and responsibilities within contemporary society. The resultant impact of this difference has been crystallized by Sager:

. . . fundamentalists attempted by credal definition and imposition to exclude from the churches . . . those whose pilgrimage of faith was leading them away from the traditional expression of entire bodies of teachings and practices which had long been regarded as sacrosanct and unchanging. [6]

Although the tenets of the fundamentalist movement had been present in American religion for a number of years, it was not until the 1920s that this movement began to receive relatively widespread support within many religious sects. Instead of being concentrated within a particular geographic region, the fundamentalist movement gained support across sectional, political, and economic lines. The universal factor that aided in the spread of the fundamentalist movement was the societal dissonance of the 1920s, a time of massive change with a concomitant increase in uncertainty as to the structure and working of an individual's world. Since it was seen that nearly every social factor was in the midst of change and reinterpretation, many individuals looked to religion to provide the necessary solid foundation for the meaning of life. Fundamentalist religion provided its adherents with a safe place away from the nagging troubles of the world,[7] a rationale summarized by Nash:

As much of the familiar intellectual terrain around them seemed to quake, a sizeable number of Americans nervously clung to old-time religion. The Bible served as a comforting, unquestioned absolute. Here was stability in an age of seeming change, security at a time of nervousness. The Rock of Ages grew in significance as investigations into the ages of rocks raised disconcerting questions. [8]

Fundamentalism as a movement reached its high-water mark at the Scopes trial in 1925 as it attempted to hold back the heretical discoveries of science and scholarship.[9] However, the trial also marked the beginning of the decline of the movement as it demonstrated that fundamentalism worked only for the past and for prior dogmas; it allowed no change or adjustment to the machinations of contemporary society. Originally seen as a great opportunity to do irreparable damage to religious modernists and "evilutionists," the fundamentalists found, instead, that it was they who were injured by the Scopes trial. Clarence Darrow's biting ridicule of William Jennings Bryan's fundamentalist doctrine was nationally generalized to a ridicule of the fundamentalist movement itself. The Scopes trial "symbolized the last major fundamentalist offensive and . . . subsequent decline in prominence."[10] The significance of the fundamentalist movement rapidly dissipated as the United States headed towards the Great Crash.

An offshoot of the societal dissonance and the fundamentalist-modernist struggle of the 1920s was the increased concern with the meaning of life and of the structural workings of man. While this issue possessed obvious philosophical import, it also contained important aspects of religious considerations that dealt with the very basic nature of man and life and the relationship of these to a supreme being. Specifically, there arose the question of man's functioning in the world: i.e., did the human organism operate as a dynamic, idiosyncratic individual or as the functioning of an advanced, flesh-made machine. Was man a machine?

While the issue of man's resemblance to a machine might seem to be of trivial importance and the sort of discussion topic designed to engender "mere rhetoric," the implications of this issue possessed crucial importance for both man and society. Indeed, the entire functioning of American society and man's relationship to that society were dependent upon the way in which man was seen as an individual. Not only would the existence and function of God be questioned by the assertion that man was but a machine, but various behavioral and legal questions would be raised by that assertion as well, a point dramatized by psychologist John B. Watson:

If man is a machine, can we punish him? Can he be naughty? Can he be nice? Have we any right to force him into any kind of conduct either good or bad? If so, what justification have we then for any kind of punishment theory whatsoever? [11]

It was this issue and its resultant implications that drew Clarence Darrow and Will Durant into public debate in early 1927.

Clarence Darrow's Position on the Issue

One of the most well-known factors of Clarence Darrow's life and philosophy was his pessimistic agnosticism and his continual refusal to accept the tenets of any Judeo-Christian religious dogma. Like many of his beliefs, Darrow secured his views of life and the existence of God from his father, Amirus Darrow, a noted agnostic and perennial iconoclast in northeastern Ohio. Because of his father's recriminations against various religious teachings and the belief that life was created from nothing by a supreme being called God, Clarence began to search elsewhere for the structure and meaning of life, and engaged in extensive reading of the biological evolutionists who achieved great prominence during his childhood. The consequential impact of this early study was noted by Ravitz:

The attention of Clarence Darrow was captured early by the Darwinian thesis and its societal and spiritual consequences . . . iconoclastic decimation of contemporary civilization became part and parcel of the ethic adopted by young Darrow. [12]

Thus, Darrow became a committed agnostic who believed that the only purpose of religion was to fool those individuals who had not carefully considered the biological creation of life.

In accord with this religious view, Darrow became, as previously suggested by Ravitz, a societal iconoclast, an individual who shot holes in the conventional societal wisdom of his time. [13] This role was best exemplified by Darrow in his activities in the Scopes trial in 1925 as he continually chipped away at the religious dogmas and beliefs of his principal legal adversary, William Jennings Bryan. Realizing that both the creation of and existence of life were concealed in the shadows of man's knowledge, Darrow indicted organized religion for suggesting that it knew the answers to the complex question of life:

. . . the riddles of existence–the problems of life, the deep heart of the universe, the cause and purpose and end of all–are mysteries as dark and inscrutable as they were eight centuries ago. [14]

Because of his convictions as to the inscrutability of the meaning and purpose of life, Darrow adopted a very pessimistic attitude toward life in general. He often questioned the very value of existence and several of his public debates considered the question, "Is Life Worth Living?", an issue upon which Darrow consistently upheld the negative position. His commitment to this philosophical position was illustrated by his remarks during a funeral address for a friend who had committed suicide: "In a moment of temporary sanity, he decided that life wasn't worth living,"[15] certainly not the most traditional of burial ceremony remarks. One advantage of this pessimistic view of life was that it allowed Darrow to accept calamitous occurrences with a minimum of emotional strain, a factor exemplified by his attitude after the Great Crash had wiped out his savings:

[Darrow] wrote later that what cushioned the shock was his lifelong pessimism. Since he was always prepared for the worst, he was never too upset when it happened . . . .[16]

However, despite his pessimism and his constant debunking of religious dogmas, Darrow found that there must be some system, some order to the functioning of human existence. One man's life could not operate within a total vacuum, devoid of all meaning and influence. Thus, Darrow came to the conclusion that life was mechanical in nature and that the human organism was nothing but a machine that was tempered by the crucial physical factors of heredity and environment. Whereas many adherents to the mechanistic view of life were caught in a dilemma over man's obvious ability to change and develop—not a common trait of machines—Darrow's view of life encompassed the variables of heredity and environment that allowed for such modifications within a mechanistic framework, a point that he illustrated in an article written for *Forum* in 1927:

Fundamentally, man is always changing, both in structure and concepts. His

mechanism and ideas are constantly acting and reacting upon each other and always reshaping the inherent man.[17]

Therefore, Clarence Darrow internalized the concept of man as machine and incorporated this idea with the scientific discoveries concerning the importance of heredity and environment in the building and functioning of man. This view of life was in keeping with his anti-religious posture of early years, and it was this philosophy of life and man's operations within the society that Darrow publicized in many of his public debates and in the courts of law.

Darrow vs. Durant

Because of the importance of the view that man functioned as a machine, the League for Public Discussion decided to host a public debate that dealt with that issue. The league chose Clarence Darrow to serve as the spokesman for mechanism and Will Durant was selected to serve as the spokesman for the anti-mechanistic point of view. Will Durant had, by 1927, established himself as the leading popularizer of philosophical treatises. After receipt of his Ph.D. from Columbia University in 1917, Durant had spent most of his time writing about philosophy, finally hitting the national scene in 1926 with the publication of *The Story of Philosophy*. Gifted with the ability to make the most complex philosophical considerations appear to be simple in nature, Will Durant's writings served to make him "the liaison officer between philosophy and the so-called man in the street."[18]

The debate between Darrow and Durant took place on January 8, 1927, in New York City's Carnegie Hall on the issue, "Is Man a Machine?" Although the specific activities of the

League for Public Discussion, the size of the audience, and other such relevant data were not recorded by the New York City newspapers,[19] it was claimed by a spokesman for the league that some two thousand people were unable to gain admission, thus indicating that the debate was staged before a very large audience.[20] Information gathered from research into the Darrow-Wheeler debate indicates that Carnegie Hall could seat in excess of three thousand persons, suggesting that the Darrow-Durant debate probably took place before an audience of this approximate number.

To serve as the chairman and timekeeper for the debate, the league selected Dr. John B. Watson, a practicing psychologist whose activities were relevant to the issue for debate. Watson had, until 1920, served as a professor of experimental and comparative psychology at Johns Hopkins University, and had been mainly concerned with behavioral studies of man. Watson left academia in 1920 to join the staff of the J. Walter Thompson advertising firm as consulting psychologist and had become a vice-president of that organization in 1924. Because of his academic and professional interests in the structural makeup of man, Dr. Watson was an excellent choice to serve as the debate's chairman.

As chairman, Watson had the responsibility of introducing both the debaters and the issue under discussion. He chose to emphasize during his opening remarks the importance of that issue:

The subject, "Is Man a Machine?" is more than a mere topic for discussion. It is a matter of vital interest to all of us; it is a matter which concerns our daily conduct . . . the debate has practical significance in our daily life.[21]

In addition, Watson chose to delineate the speaking burdens that he felt the debaters should attempt to meet in dealing with the debate issue:

I do feel that the speakers tonight should take this question rather logically, should give us some hard facts, should give us some kind of definitions . . . . We want to keep our common sense because we feel that we are able to judge facts and, at any rate, to scrutinize their logical positions.[22]

Thus, with the call for a logical analysis of man's purported mechanistic structure, Watson turned over the discussion to the debaters. Although it has been standard forensic practice to begin each debate with the affirmative presentation, the Darrow-Durant confrontation broke tradition, and Will Durant's negative address was delivered first. Durant was given three periods of speaking time that totalled sixty minutes; Darrow was given two speaking periods that totalled the same. Thus, unlike the standard debate practice, the negative spokesman both initiated and closed the debate.

Will Durant's Argumentation and Strategy

It should be remembered that the topic for this debate posed a particular problem for both Darrow and Durant. "Is Man a Machine?" is a proposition of fact, a statement of objective certainty that called for very careful delineation of specific definitions of terms. Within that debate question, the term "machine" served as the term that most necessitated a clear definition that would be accepted by both debaters. A perusal of the major arguments of both Darrow and Durant indicate that the definitions of "machine" offered by each speaker did not mesh: they were not talking about

Table IV   Major Arguments in the Darrow-Durant Debate

Clarence Darrow	Will Durant
Machine: that which can change one form of energy into another	Machine: must be able to explain all human behavior
Durant cannot prove that man is not a machine	Darrow is begging the question
Man is probably a machine	Concept of mechanism is being changed in most sciences
Man more nearly resembles a machine than anything else	Man possesses unmechanical spontaneity —locomotion —digestion —growth —regeneration
One can discover everything that is in man	
Everything done by man is performed as a machine	This concept is a defensive reaction

the same idea or concept (see Table IV). This difference in definition served to do damage to the entire structure of the debate in that one's arguments, designed to meet the definition he himself offered, often did not apply to the arguments offered by his debate opponent who labored under another definition.

This problem can be illustrated by the juxtaposition of the two definitions of "machine" offered by the debaters. In beginning his first negative presentation, Will Durant offered the following definition to clarify the issues within the debate:

. . . I shall interpret the term machine, or (as the theory of living machines is called in philosophy) the theory of mechanism, as meaning that man and all living things are mechanical in the sense that their behavior can be entirely explained in mechanical terms, on the principles that seem to hold good in industry, in physics, and in chemistry. [23]

Thus, according to Durant, "machine" was defined as that which could be explained in mechanical

terms and that which served to explain all human behavior.

Careful consideration of Durant's definition will reveal that not only did it carefully delimit the perimeters which he desired to place around the topic but also that it placed an immense burden upon the affirmative speaker. Note that Durant claimed that "mechanism" must *entirely* explain all of human behavior, a massive burden of proof that most probably would be impossible to meet within any issue of debate. By this definition, it was Darrow's responsibility to explain every idiosyncratic behavioral expression that man had consummated since the beginning of recorded history. Therefore, it was not surprising to find that Darrow did not accept this definition, but instead, offered another definition of his own.

Clarence Darrow offered the following definition:

One definition of a machine that appeals to me as pretty good is this: 'An apparatus so designed that it can change one kind of energy to another for a purpose.'... What do we know about the human machine? We know that it takes one form of energy and transposes it into another. [24]

Thus, Darrow's definition of "machine" encompassed only the major concept of energy reformation, that any system or organism that operated upon the power derived from the rechanneling of various energy sources could be called mechanical in nature. Therefore, Darrow's definition had little, if anything, to do with the definition offered by Durant. Darrow was concerned with an internal process of conversion; Durant was concerned with the external process of overt behavior. Neither debater based his ultimate position upon a definition of terms that was compatible with the operative definitions of his opponent. The debate, therefore, progressed much like the conversation between two people speaking different languages, and the resultant product suffered because of this difference.

This definitional difference served to illustrate the inherent difficulties within a proposition of fact for public debate. Unless both debaters agree upon the fact to be disputed, there will be a minimum of clash, and the audience will suffer. A member of the Darrow-Durant debate audience could have agreed with both of the speakers and never have reached any sort of conclusion about the topic under discussion, a very unfortunate circumstance within any public confrontation. This definitional difference also illustrated the negligence of the debate's chairman in failing to step in and to force some sort of definitional agreement between Darrow and Durant. If Dr. Watson had done this, it is quite conceivable that the quality of the debate could have been improved, at least the two debaters would have been talking about the same concept and audience comprehension would have been aided.

After the presentation of his definition of "machine," Durant proceeded to a brief consideration of the creation of the concept that man was a machine. Basically, Durant claimed that it was the Industrial Revolution that created the concept advocated by Darrow, and he inferred that this had not been a fortunate occurrence:

It was the Industrial Revolution that filled the world with the strange notion that man is a machine. For first of all it accustomed the mind to dealing with machines and induced it more and more to think of causes not as biological, but as mechanical .... The world, which had once been a picture of growing plants and wilful children, of loving mothers and ambitious men, became for the modern mind a vast array of mechanisms, from the planets that circled mechanically around the sun to the crowds that flocked mechanically to be in at the death of a moving-picture star. [25]

The strength of this argument lay not in its particular content but with the scene of mechanism that was created. Durant painted a picture that showed men to be stumbling about like automatons, a situation both desired and created by those who espoused the concept that man was a machine. In short, Durant attempted to gain a strategic advantage through the creation of the impression that Darrow served as the spokesman for those who were attempting to depersonalize man and society, thereby creating a world that would not be a pleasant one in which to live.

From this point, Durant moved to two quick indictments of philosophical mechanism that were designed to strengthen his overall position. First, he claimed that the concept of mechanism was rapidly becoming an outmoded scientific construct:

It may comfort you to know that at the very moment when the theory of mechanism has reached down into popular favor, it is being abandoned in a great many of the sciences, in biology (not in psychology), in physiology, even in physics itself. [26]

Not only would this argument serve as support for Durant's position that the credibility of mechanism was rapidly diminishing, it would also serve to cut out any scientific argument of mechanism that Darrow might be disposed to offer. In most of his public utterances, Darrow consistently took the role of spokesman for those enlightened interests that had progressed because of the internalization of recent scientific inquiry. In this case, Durant denied Darrow the ability to assume that role by contending that the general body of science refused to accept the theory of mechanism. [27]

Second, Durant contended that the concept of mechanism was nothing more than a defensive reaction to theology:

[Mechanism] is a conception that comes to one only in an effort to leap back as far as possible from the theological hobgoblins of our youth. It is a defense reaction, and once we have ceased to fear the recrudescence of theology in our own souls we shall be freer and clearer in recognizing the shortcomings of this mechanical theory. [28]

Again, we have an argument that was of particular significance to Darrow. The affirmative speaker's well-known agnosticism and anti-theological stance were made to order for this argument that suggested that mechanism was an offshoot of the fear of theology. It became apparent by Durant's first rebuttal period that he did not intend to press this particular argument, because he reacted most negatively to Darrow's refutation of religious concepts within his first speech: "I resent . . . the effort to drag religion into the debate and to compel me to defend things which are not at issue!"[29] Of course, Durant had been the initiator of this issue, but his reaction to Darrow's extension of the theological point indicated that the only purpose of this argument was to throw a pointed barb at Darrow's general philosophy of life. Durant was not prepared to extend the argument beyond that point.

With over one-third of his speaking time elapsed, Durant proceeded to argue what he believed man to be. The remainder of his address was spent in developing this concept that he crystallized at the beginning of this argument:

Let us do our own thinking and face the phenomena directly for ourselves. Let us observe the unmechanical spontaneity, and purposiveness and selectiveness of life in locomotion, in digestion, in growth, in regeneration, in reproduction, in consciousness, and in genius. [30]

The crucial part of the foregoing statement is the phrase "unmechanical spontaneity," because that served as the major argument with which Durant chose to do battle with mechanistic theory. Stated simply, Durant charged that man was idiosyncratic, highly individualistic in his actions, thereby serving as literal living proof that man was not machine-like. Using examples drawn from man's locomotive, digestive, growth, regenerative, reproductive, conscious, and mental abilities, Durant concluded that the very actions that characterized man served as *prima facie* proof that man was not mechanical in nature, but was dynamic and spontaneous in his motivations and actions. The creative power of man, concluded Durant, proved that man was not a machine. After all, although machines could act, they certainly could not create. Because of man's creative power, he was more than just a mere machine:

Man, the supposed machine, invents and operates machines, and craves beauty, and seeks truth, and creates social order, and rises to the loftiest reaches of morality and love. [31]

Man was, therefore, not a machine; man was man.

Clarence Darrow's Argumentation and Strategy

Clarence Darrow possessed an unenviable position within the debate with Will Durant. First, as the affirmative speaker, his duty was to uphold the burden of proof that, in fact, man was a machine. Beyond that, moreover, because Durant spoke first during the constructive periods, Darrow also had the responsibility to respond to Durant's line of argumentation. Thus, the reversal of speaking positions literally doubled Darrow's speaking responsibilities within his first affirmative presentation.

In support of his mechanistic position and in direct refutation of Durant's position, Darrow began his presentation by claiming that Durant had been unable to prove that man was not a machine:

If one seriously does not believe that man is a machine, then it is up to him as a matter of fairness to tell us what man is–if he can–which he can't. [32]

Durant responded to this argument by claiming that Darrow was begging the question, that his argument assumed the existence of the fact that was, in reality, the disputed issue under discussion. [33] While Durant

was correct in his response to Darrow's argument, he could have gone further and accused Darrow of a failure to uphold his burden of proof to substantiate the claim that man was a machine. Within the division of responsibilities in any debate, it is the duty of the affirmative to rationalize the existence of the debate topic: in this instance, that man functioned as a mechanical organism. [34] Darrow refused to uphold this burden; he even admitted that he could not uphold this burden by saying, "I will be honest with you in this matter. I cannot prove to you that man is a machine." [35] Thus, Darrow dropped his responsibility of the burden of proof and unsuccessfully attempted to thrust this burden upon his opponent. Durant refused to shoulder this affirmative responsibility and returned it to where it belonged—right in Darrow's lap.

After dropping the burden of proof, Darrow then proceeded to state four major lines of argument in support of the debate topic. First, he claimed that man was probably a machine:

What I do contend is this: that the manifestation of the human machine and of living organisms is very like unto what we know as a machine, and that if we could find it all out we would probably find that everything had a mechanistic origin. [36]

Note that Darrow's position of support is based upon an unknown probability. He admitted that he could not prove that man was a machine; his position was based upon a nonspecified futuristic proof that probably would support his position. While the use of futuristic probability as a statement of proof can serve viably within many argumentative contexts, it cannot adequately serve as a replacement for the maintenance of the burden of proof. Instead, futuristic proof within this context serves only to aid Durant's contentions at the expense of Darrow's mechanistic theory.

Second, Darrow extended this argument of futuristic probability by claiming that man more nearly resembled a machine than anything else:

[Science] has found enough to justify the conclusion that man more nearly resembles a machine than he resembles a ghost carrying around a body for a time, much more nearly than he resembles something that no scientist even dares to talk about . . . .[37]

It was, thus, at this point that Darrow reacted to the issue of "theological defense reaction" that had been introduced by Durant. Substitution of the word "soul" for "ghost" in the foregoing statement would make Darrow's statement clearer, but the intent of the argument would remain the same. Durant refused to continue argumentation along theological lines of thought, and this argument was effectively dropped from the remainder of the debate.

Third, Darrow contended that man should be considered a machine because man's functions were performed as if he were a machine:

Is there anything that a man presents in his conduct, in his actions, in the uses of his abilities, that isn't performed in exactly the same way as a machine? I think there is not.[38]

Here we have an incredibly weak argument. Darrow attempted to prove his position through literal analogy, but this argument, in and of itself, demonstrated the general argumentative weakness of his entire position. To argue that man should be considered a machine because he resembled a machine in his actions would be equivalent to arguing that man should be considered a bear because both can walk on two legs, eat berries, and growl. In short, similarity does not necessarily mean that any two objects are the same, but that is exactly what Darrow attempted to argue. Durant responded to this argument by indignantly labelling the comparison as "childish" in nature, but he never explained why he believed Darrow's argument to be absurd. Had he taken the time to explain the fallacious structure of the analogy, Durant would have presented a much more effective piece of refutation to this argument.

Finally, Darrow argued that man was a machine because one could discover everything that was within a man:

When it comes to man you can find out every single thing that is in him. There isn't a single thing in him you can't buy at the drug store for about ninety-five cents, and a good many of them aren't worth it at that![39]

The impetus for this argument probably sprang from Durant's continual reiteration that man was not a machine because of his great genius and creative power. Thus, Darrow's argument would be designed to suggest that, like a machine, man could be broken down into his component parts, studied, and analyzed. However, Durant refused to accept this comparison, arguing that there was no way that man's creative abilities could be seen, or held, or studied. According to Durant, it was this particular power of life that most notably distinguished man from machines.[40] This argument remained virtually intact throughout the remainder of the debate with both Darrow and Durant generally repeating their initial lines of argumentation and not extending their analyses to include the reasoning of the opposition.

Darrow vs. Durant: Evaluation

The debate between Clarence Darrow and Will Durant aptly demonstrated the inherent dangers involved in debating a proposition of fact. As noted previously, to be able to debate effectively such a proposition, there must be some sort of consensus between the debaters as to exactly what is being debated. In this case, the two widely differing definitions of "machine" offered by Darrow and Durant illustrated that they were not actually dealing with the same kind of concept, that they were not talking about the same conceptual framework. The problem posed by such a situation is that it would be possible to accept both debaters' major lines of arguments without reaching any sort of definitive conclusion. For example, it was quite possible that any member of the audience could have agreed with Darrow that man was machine-like in his actions and, at the same time, could have agreed with Durant that man possessed the creative power of genius not found in machines. Thus, the major arguments were not necessarily exclusionary: that is, one argument by the negative did not necessarily negate an argument by the affirmative and *vice versa*. Had the chairman of the debate decided to step in to force the debaters to accept a common definition of machine, he might have been able to force them to come to terms with one another's arguments, but he did not do that. Thus, the quality of the debate suffered as Darrow and Durant were speaking on two different argumentative and conceptual planes.

Nonetheless, despite the lack of agreement on definitions of terms, a judgment of the debate may still be rendered. Specifically, Clarence Darrow would have to be indicted for his overt failure to uphold the burden of proof of the proposition that was incumbent upon his position as the debate's affirmative speaker. Although it was unusual and refreshing, to say the least, to see an affirmative speaker admit that he was unable to prove conclusively the position he was defending, it certainly did not serve his overall strategy and line of argumentation very well. Instead, such an admission immediately placed Darrow upon the defensive, forced to respond to the argumentative thrusts of Durant, when it has been the normal practice within debate to have the second speaker force the first speaker to be on the defensive. Thus, from the start, Darrow was at a strategic disadvantage, and the remainder of the debate saw Durant taking the lead in pressing this advantage.

In addition, Darrow allowed the major line of Durant's argumentation to stand unrefuted. Durant had claimed that the major difference between man and machine was man's unmechanical spontaneity as exemplified by man's locomotive, digestive, growth, and regenerative capabilities. Darrow did not directly deal with this general argument nor its supportive substructure. Instead, he weakly argued that man should be considered a machine because man somewhat resembled a machine, an argument that was inherently deficient in and of itself and an argument that failed to deal with the thrust of Durant's line of argumentation.

Therefore, because of Darrow's failure to uphold the burden of proof of the proposition and because of his inability to deal directly and adequately with the major line of argumentation offered by Durant, this writer would conclude that the decision of this debate must be awarded to Will Durant. Darrow lost the debate because of his own argumentative shortcomings rather than because of the power and force of Durant's lines of argumentation. Had Darrow been able to uphold the burden of proof, the result might have been different, but he did not, and the ultimate result of the debate was foretold in the first three minutes of Darrow's opening speech.

Unfortunately, no audience vote was taken at the conclusion of the debate, so there is no record as to any audience decision on the debate's victor. However, one factor appears to be fairly certain. In his introductory remarks to the debate, Dr. John B. Watson had stated that this debate "will unquestionably go down in history as one of the great debates of all time."[41] Some two hours after making this statement, it is fairly certain that Watson was horribly disappointed.

Footnotes

[1] Roderick Nash, *The Nervous Generation: American Thought, 1917-1930* (Chicago, 1970), p. v.

[2] Allan H. Sager, "Modernists and Fundamentalists Debate Restraints on Freedom," in *America in Controversy*, edited by DeWitte Holland (Dubuque, 1973), p. 296.

[3] Paul A. Carter, *The Decline and Revival of the Social Gospel: Social and Political Liberalism in American Protestant Churches, 1920-1940* (Ithaca, 1954), p. 4.

[4] *Ibid.*, p. 48.

[5] Willard H. Smith, "William Jennings Bryan and the Social Gospel," *Journal of American History*, LIII (June, 1966), p. 56

[6] Sager, pp. 281-282.

[7] Carter, p. 57.

[8] Nash, p. 148.

[9] Carter, p. 46.

[10] Sager, p. 304.

[11] Clarence Darrow and Will Durant, *Are We Machines?* (Girard, 1928), p. 11.

[12] Abe C. Ravitz, *Clarence Darrow and the American Literary Tradition* (Cleveland, 1962), p. xi.

[13] This view of Darrow is also supported by Irving Stone, *Clarence Darrow for the Defense* (Garden City, 1941), pp. 77-80; and Lawrence W. Levine, *Defender of the Faith* (New York, 1965), p. 348.

[14] Clarence Darrow, "The Human Being's World," in *A Preface to the Universe*, edited by Baker Brownell (New York, 1929), p. 70.

[15] Cited in Arthur Garfield Hays, *City Lawyer* (New York, 1942), p. 440.

[16] Miriam Gurko, *Clarence Darrow* (New York, 1965), p. 246.

[17] Clarence Darrow, "Is Man Fundamentally Dishonest?", *Forum*, LXXVIII (December, 1927), p. 884.

[18] *The National Cyclopedia of American Biography*, 1930, C, p. 474.

[19] In its chronological index, the *New York Times* has a listing for an article

dealing with the Darrow-Durant debate. See the *New York Times*, January 9, 1927, II, p. 6. However, no such article could be found by this writer. Subsequent investigation into this matter by the staff of the Chicago Public Library revealed no *Times* article on the Darrow-Durant debate.

20 Darrow and Durant, p. 5.

21 *Ibid.*, pp. 7-8.

22 *Ibid.*, pp. 9-11.

23 *Ibid.*, pp. 12-13.

24 *Ibid.*, p. 34.

25 *Ibid.*, pp. 13-14.

26 *Ibid.*, pp. 17-18.

27 Darrow's assumption of the role of scientific spokesman is easily noted in the debate with Judge Talley on capital punishment. Also, see Darrow's pronouncements in the Loeb-Leopold case and the Scopes trial.

28 Darrow and Durant, pp. 19-20.

29 *Ibid.*, p. 45.

30 *Ibid.*, p. 20.

31 *Ibid.*, p. 28.

32 *Ibid.*, p. 33.

33 *Ibid.*, p. 47.

34 Any standard debate text explicitly points out that he who affirms the proposition under discussion has the responsibility of upholding the burden of proof. That is, the affirmative speaker must present a credible case that forces the negative speaker to respond to that case.

35 Darrow and Durant, p. 33.

36 *Ibid.*

37 *Ibid.*, p. 36.

38 *Ibid.*, p. 37.

39 *Ibid.*, p. 41.

40 *Ibid.*, p. 49.

41 *Ibid.*, p. 7.

Chapter Six

Immigration

Restriction upon the immigration of foreign peoples into the United States had its roots in the initial laws adopted under the Alien Act of 1798 during President John Adams's administration. However, after the expiration of the Alien Act in 1800, the United States virtually had no immigration restriction policy for the next seventy-five years. Despite the fact that some individual states adopted restrictions, the Supreme Court ruled that such laws were unconstitutional in that only the federal government possessed the legal right to limit the flow of immigrants.[1] Thus, throughout the major growth period of the American nation, immigrants were generally allowed to enter the United States at their own will, and little was done to restrict this flow.

However, by 1875, there had arisen great concern over such an unrestricted immigration policy and, gradually, specific constraints were placed upon potential immigrants to control more carefully the flow of new peoples into the United States. Federal laws of 1875 and 1882 placed a ban upon the immigration of "undesirables" into this country—prostitutes, convicted criminals, and people who carried contagious diseases. Yet many individuals believed that even greater restrictions should have been implemented. Private organizations, such as the Immigration Restriction League in Boston, began to clamor for legislation that would curtail the immigration of political undesirables into the United States. Under the pressure of such organizations, the Congress adopted the Immigration

Law of 1903 that made inadmissible those individuals who were:

. . . anarchists, or persons who believe in, or advocate the overthrow by force or violence of the Government of the United States, or of all government, or of all forms of law, or the assassination of public officials. [2]

Thus, within a span of less than thirty years, the United States had moved from being a nation with no restrictive immigration policy to one that placed careful restrictions upon the social and political beliefs and activities of its potential immigrants.

This anti-immigration attitude was also fueled by labor interests who feared the competition of relatively cheap labor from foreign shores. This fear was especially manifested on America's West Coast, where the continued immigration of various Oriental laborers posed a threat to the American workingman living in that area. To deal with this perceived problem, President Theodore Roosevelt effectuated the "Gentlemen's Agreement" in 1907 and 1908 that saw Japan capitulate to the American position to restrict the numbers of people who would be allowed to emigrate to the United States. Despite this agreement, Congress adopted, over President Woodrow Wilson's veto, the Immigration Act of 1917 that imposed a stringent literacy requirement designed to curtail even further Oriental immigration. By the time of American involvement in the First World War, therefore, the United States had compiled a number of restrictive immigration policies that had effectively begun to limit the previously unrestricted flow of immigrants into "the land of opportunity."

The Impact of the First World War

American experience during the First World War served to instill a desire for increased restriction upon immigration. During the war, the people of the United States had been made aware of the dangers of foreign subversion and sabotage, and the activities of George Creel's Committee on Public Information created the impression that any foreign influence was potentially dangerous to the security of the nation. Thus, to deal with this wartime threat, the American people were conditioned and propagandized to deal immediately with the foreign danger from within, and this was not a trait that was to end with the cessation of hostilities.[3]

Because the domestic front had created the fear of any person or idea that was alien to the United States, postwar policy *vis-a-vis* immigration was directly affected by wartime attitudes.[4] The Bolshevik Revolution had effectively withdrawn Russia from involvement in the war against the Central Powers and, because of this one factor alone, had created an anti-communist feeling amongst the American people. In addition, it was feared that the Bolsheviki desired to foment internal rebellion within the United States. To combat this perceived menace, the federal government and numerous state agencies launched a vigorous anti-revolutionary campaign to circumscribe radical activities in the months immediately following the war. Suppression of unpopular beliefs and ideas had been sanctioned during the war, and this suppression continued into the third decade of the twentieth century as a direct offshoot from that wartime experience.[5]

The unfortunate consequence of this fear of foreign subversion and revolution was that it was extended to include all alien concepts and individuals. The suppression of German and Bolshevik revolutionaries was expanded to encompass all foreigners, because, within the American mind, the terms "alien" and "radical" had become synonymous.[6] Thus, all immigrants were considered to be potential threats to the peace and security of the United States, and the same basic mentality that had created an anti-German and anti-Bolshevik hysteria served to create an anti-immigration posture:

The 1920s . . . were really not so different from the preceding decade. The overt delirium had subsided and the techniques of repression had changed. On the other hand, the ideological framework was certainly the same; perhaps it had even become more uncompromisingly anti-radical.[7]

Therefore, because of the extension of the fear of foreign revolutionaries that sprang from the American experience during the First World War, the United States embarked upon a policy of increased immigration restriction throughout the 1920s. The national legislation that was created during this time period would be the primary immigration legislation that would control such matters until the adoption of the Immigration and Nationality Act of 1952.

However, it would be erroneous to believe that the anti-immigration policies of the 1920s stemmed entirely from the fear of internal revolution. On the contrary, three other factors were significant in the creation of this national policy. First, there was the continued fear on the part of labor interests of the impact of immigration upon the American economy and the livelihood of the

American workingman. Although Oriental immigration had been checked in the main by the Immigration Law of 1917, there was continued fear of the impact of other peoples upon the job market. Thus, this fear provided still another rationale for the restriction of immigration, a rationale that was expressed by President Coolidge in his defense of the highly restrictive Immigration Quota Act of 1924:

[The law] seeks to shield our wage earners from the disastrous competition of a great influx of foreign peoples. This has been done by the restrictive immigration law. This saves the American job for the American workmen. . . . We must maintain our own economic position, we must defend our own national integrity. [8]

Because it was felt that continued immigration at pre-First World War levels would eventually cost Americans their jobs and their prosperous economy, it was argued that immigration had to be curtailed to prevent an erosion of the national economy by cheap, unskilled foreign labor. Therefore, the immigration restrictions of the 1920s had an economic as well as an ideological basis for existence.

Second, perceived differences in lifestyles and customs between immigrants and natives created another rationale for restrictive immigration policies. While the United States had opened her doors to immigrants during most of the nineteenth century upon the assumption that this country was the great "melting pot" that forged one people from many different racial stocks, this assumption was widely castigated during the 1920s. Instead of melting into the mainstream of American life, it was argued, the immigrants continued to practice lifestyles and customs that were essentially foreign to the American nation. Therefore, to improve this

process, immigration should be significantly curbed to allow the existing foreign element within the country adequate time to be "Americanized" in the great melting pot, an argument expressed by United States Senator Wesley L. Jones of Washington: "I believe that we ought to stop immigration until we get those who are here fully and thoroughly assimilated . . . ." [9] This argument carried great weight for the urbanite who saw at close hand the growth of the various ethnic ghettos within large cities, ghettos that carried on Old World customs in the heart of metropolitan America.

Although the ruralite did not come face to face with this assimilation problem too often, he, too, was upset with the failure to Americanize the immigrants for two separate reasons as suggested by Kirschner:

. . . they resisted assimilation by rushing to their own people as soon as they got off the boat. In short, they were clannish, and the ruralite found this distasteful for two reasons . . . it seemed to imply a rejection of the American way of life . . . [and] the foreigner's apparent exclusiveness only packed more closely the slums that lent such a vile tone to urban life. [10]

Thus, the immigrant found himself condemned for his desire in seeking security among his own people upon arrival and for his association with the urban areas, areas that were bogeymen to the rural mentality.

Third, a restrictive immigration policy was rationalized on the data proffered by eugenicists who proclaimed that there were inherent racial qualities within mankind that caused some racial stocks to be superior or inferior to others. Oscar Handlin has provided the description and importance of the works produced by those who held this position of biological polarity:

A succession of books . . . demonstrated that flaws in the biological constitution of various groups of immigrants were responsible for every evil that beset the country—for pauperism, for the low birth rate of natives, for economic depressions, for class divisions, for prostitution and homosexuality, and for the appearance of city slums. [11]

One of the popular eugenicists during the 1920s was Dr. Lothrop Stoddard, and his best-selling work, *The Rising Tide of Color*, published in 1920, exemplified the claim that there were obvious dichotomies among racial stocks with the concomitant conclusion that the Caucasian race was the most superior. Utilizing a large amount of statistical analysis, Stoddard contended that the white race was the most industrious and intelligent race and that, within the white race, the Nordics, made up of people from northern and western Europe and the majority of those living within the United States, were the superior stock:

. . . the white race divides into three main sub-species—the Nordics, and Alpines, and the Mediterraneans. All three are good stocks, ranking in generic worth well above the various colored races. However, there seems to be no question that the Nordic is far and away the most valuable type . . . . The Nordic is 'The Great Race.' [12]

Therefore, because it was contended that there existed significant differences between racial stocks, anti-immigration forces claimed that immigration had to be greatly curtailed to maintain the purity of the American racial composition. Thus, the restrictive immigration policy of the United States had a tint of racism during the 1920s. [13]

The Immigration Law of 1924

Because of the forementioned pressures, agitation for further immigration restriction increased as the United States entered the 1920s. In 1921, the first quantitative restriction was placed upon immigrant groups with the Quota Law of 1921, a statute that:

. . . limited the number of aliens of any nationality entering the United States to three per cent of foreign-born persons of that nationality who had lived in the United States in 1910. Under this law approximately 350,000 aliens were permitted to enter each year as quota immigrants, mostly from Northern and Western Europe. [14]

Thus, for the first time, immigration policy set a specific maximum number of potential immigrants who could enter this country on a yearly basis. As Auerbach has noted, the various nationality quotas were designed in such a way so as to maximize the immigration of Nordics at the expense of other racial stocks, thereby institutionalizing the biological racism advocated by the eugenicists.

Despite this legislation, agitation for further immigration restriction continued, resulting in the adoption of the Immigration Quota Act of 1924, the most restrictive of all immigration policies up to that time. This law contained two major provisions of importance. First, it established quota provisions similar to the Quota Law of 1921, except that the new law utilized the year 1890 as the base year upon which the various quotas were to be set. This was an important difference, because moving the base year back increased the number of potential Nordic immigrants and greatly diminished the number of potential immigrants from central and southern Europe. Most of the Mediterranean countries were given extremely low quotas, thereby assuring that the vast majority of immigrants would be members of Stoddard's "Great Race." Second, the Immigration

Quota Act of 1924 contained the provision of the implementation of the "National Origins Quota System" in 1929, whereby immigration was controlled by a quota system that was based upon the relationship of 150,000 inhabitants of the United States in 1920. This complex system went even further in restricting overall immigration, a factor that has been demonstrated by the perusal of the yearly number of immigrants who came to the United States during the enforcement of this law. For example, in the year before the implementation of the 1924 law, some 706,896 immigrants entered the United States; in 1925 the number dropped to 294,314; and in 1934, ten years after the law's adoption, immigration statistics stood at 29,470.[15] Within the period of one decade, then, immigration to the United States had been cut by ninety-five percent.

The popularity of such stringent restrictions was shown in the final congressional vote upon the Immigration Quota Act of 1924. Despite the lobbying of such pro-immigration groups as the National Liberal Immigration League, the Senate adopted the law by a vote of sixty-nine to nine; the House of Representatives voted favorably three-hundred-eight to fifty-eight.[16] On July 1, 1924, President Calvin Coolidge declared the law to be in force and said, "America must be kept American,"[17] thereby legitimizing the various social, racial, and economic arguments that had called for immigration restriction. The *New York Times* editorially approved the new law, concluding that "the smaller number of those of foreign tongue should help us to catch up in bringing all the people of America to understand and use one language."[18] But Oscar Handlin has contended that the goals of this immigration

policy went unmet because the resident aliens responded defensively to this attempt to force Americanization:

. . . restriction intensified the group consciousness of the immigrant peoples. The number of associations and the scope of their activity continued to increase. These still served the old functions of sociability and insurance. But in addition they became instruments of defense against the overt hostility of the society that rejected their members.[19]

This defensive reaction worked counterproductively to the aims of restrictive immigration and intensified the differences between the racial and ethnic groups within the United States. To the resident alien and the potential immigrant, President Coolidge's statement that America had preserved the "equality of opportunity" concept upon which this country had been founded must have seemed like a glittering generalization that applied only to native-born citizens.[20] Because of various political, economic, social, and biological ideas, immigrants were generally denied access to this so-called equalized opportunity, and this national desire to restrict immigration would be continued through the McCarthy era of the 1950s.

Clarence Darrow's Position on the Issue

Clarence Darrow's attitude toward immigration restriction was largely based upon his general attitude of philosophical humanism. Darrow disliked governmental restrictions upon the freedom of speech and action of the individual, and it was this philosophy that characterized his approach toward immigration policy. Although immigration policy *per se* was not one of Darrow's major causes, the continual advocacy of human freedom was, and it was within this context that Darrow viewed the restrictive immigration laws of the 1920s.

The national consciousness that created massive immigration restriction sprang from a patriotic nativism that had been developed during the First World War, and Darrow constantly fought against the excesses of this nativism. Darrow's sarcastic condemnation of what Nash has called "nervous nativism" was captured by Darrow's long-time friend and associate, Arthur Garfield Hays:

. . . optimism is not justified. The aspirations of the 'Founding Fathers' were formed on high ideals—and one may well question whether this idealism is now existent. Has it not become the bunk? Order has become the fetish; prosperity is its handmaiden; respectability its emblem. Conformity is the watchword. Production, possessions, material success, the end . . . . A dominating complacence, a comfortable obliviousness, an ignorant pretense, mark the Babbittry of those who govern. This is the best of all possible worlds; mine is the best country in the world; mine is the best state in the country; my city is the best city in the state; my school is the best school in the city. Rah! Rah! Rah! Rotary![21]

Darrow's unhappiness with the patriotic excesses of the 1920s was combined with his oft-expressed view that business capital interests had too much sway over public social policy. In his view, the wealthy capitalists were responsible for many of the ills that plagued society, including the patriotic hysteria of the decade. Unlike most others who were concerned with organized labor's activities regarding immigration policy, Darrow preferred to indict those capitalists who, he claimed, opposed liberal immigration policies in an attempt to

maintain the *status quo*. By so doing, Darrow asserted that the business interests could control society and the economy to the betterment of capital at the expense of the workingman. Therefore, national immigration policy was seen by Darrow as but another area wherein elitists were motivated by the goal of societal stagnation, not by societal betterment.

Darrow vs. Stoddard

Public agitation over immigration policy remained fairly constant throughout the early years of the 1920s, then tapered off as the Immigration Quota Act of 1924 became law and was implemented. Not only were fewer immigrants admitted to the United States under the new policy, but more deportations were recorded as well. Between 1924, the year that the new policy was enforced, and 1929, the year of the Darrow-Stoddard debate, deportation of domestic aliens increased over five hundred percent, totalling some 38,796 in 1929, the largest number of deportations until the midpoint of the Second World War.[22] For the entire decade of the 1920s, nearly 200,000 aliens were excluded from entering the United States by the restrictive immigration policy and over 160,000 aliens were deported, the highest such numbers for any decade in the history of the United States.

Concern with immigration policy increased again as the time for the implementation of the "National Origins Quota System" neared in late 1928. Recognizing this public interest, the League for Public Discussion hosted another public debate upon a timely social issue, again selecting Clarence Darrow as one of the major verbal combatants. To oppose the Chicago lawyer in a debate on immigration policy, the

league selected Dr. Lothrop Stoddard, a well-known advocate of biological eugenicism and restrictive immigration policies.

Lothrop Stoddard had as fine a formal education as anyone could have desired: bachelor's, master's, and doctoral degrees from Harvard and a Doctor of Laws degree from Boston University. Stoddard achieved fame as a writer, magazine editor, and radio journalist, and he authored some twenty-three books that dealt with world affairs.[23] Two of his works dealt directly with issues inherent in the questions surrounding immigration policy, and these works demonstrated that Stoddard possessed an elitist view of the proper governing of men as well as a naked fear that world events might eventually become dictated by nonwhite peoples.

To understand Lothrop Stoddard's brand of racism, it must be recognized that, first, Stoddard was an overt white supremacist who believed that the colored or nonwhite peoples were not much better than savages, a point exemplified in the following citation from *The Revolt Against Civilization*:

Racial impoverishment is the plague of civilization. This insidious disease, with its twin symptoms the extirpation of superior strains and the multiplication of inferiors, has ravaged humanity like a consuming fire, reducing the proudest societies to charred and squalid ruin . . . . The rarity of mental as compared with physical superiority in the human species is seen on every hand. Existing savage and barbarian races of a demonstrably low average level of intelligence, like the negroes, are physically vigorous . . . . The same is true of intellectually decadent peoples like those about the Mediterranean, whose loss of ancient mental greatness has been accompanied by no corresponding physical decline.[24]

Therefore, according to Stoddard, because of the superiority of the white race and the mental depravity of the nonwhite races, it was imperative that everything possible be done to maintain the international control of power in the hands of the white race, otherwise civilization would collapse under the pressures of the nonwhite races, causing "social sterilization and ultimate racial extinction."[25]

However, it must be remembered that Stoddard also saw distinctions amongst the racial stocks of the white race itself. Although he claimed that the three white races, the Nordics, the Alpines, and the Mediterraneans, were superior to any and all of the nonwhite races, Stoddard made it clear that the Nordics were the best of the best. Thus, he desired the United States to be a land populated mainly by those of the Nordic stock, but he found that his "Great Race" was losing ground throughout much of the country:

Our country, originally settled almost exclusively by Nordics, was toward the close of the nineteenth century invaded by hordes of immigrant Alpines and Mediterraneans, not to mention Asiatic elements like Levantines and Jews. As a result, the Nordic native American has been crowded out with amazing rapidity by these swarming, prolific aliens, and after two short generations he has in many of our urban areas become almost extinct.[26]

Therefore, to prevent the further decline of American society and civilization, Stoddard called for extremely stringent immigration policies that would allow only those peoples of the Nordic stock to enter the United States, thus achieving his goal of "race betterment." Because of his oft-stated anti-immigration positions, Stoddard served as the logical opponent for Darrow's theorizing on the propriety of American immigration policy.

The League for Public Discussion scheduled the debate for early 1929 in New York City. Although no New York City or Chicago newspaper provided coverage of either the preparation for or the culmination of the debate, material from the debate transcript indicated that it was staged before a fairly large audience, probably at either the Manhattan Opera House or Carnegie Hall, and that the debate took place during the evening hours. No specific reference could be found that provided the exact date of the debate, although this writer has hypothesized that the confrontation probably occurred during either February or March of 1929 because the debaters' speeches were published by the Haldeman-Julius Company in April of that year.

Each speaker was given a total of one hour of speaking time in which to support his respective position upon the debate topic, "Resolved: that the immigration law discriminating in favor of the races of northern Europe as opposed to those of southern Europe is an advantage to the United States." Dr. Stoddard upheld the affirmative position, while Clarence Darrow assumed the negative.

Lothrop Stoddard's Lines of Argumentation and Strategy

As in the public debates with Judge Talley and Wayne Wheeler, the debate proposition centered upon a topic of value, especially that part which determined whether or not the current immigration policy was an "advantage" to the United States. Therefore, to provide a meaningful clash of ideas, the concept of advantageousness required careful definition. Dr. Stoddard, as the affirmative speaker, had the initial responsibility of providing this needed clarity, and he did so by operationally defining the topic to include "the interest of the people of the United States as a whole."[27] Thus, if a policy were to the benefit of the people as a whole, then such a policy would be considered advantageous. Darrow did not dispute this operational definition; instead, he simply avoided it in indicting Stoddard for his narrow nativist philosophy throughout the debate. As will be discovered later, Stoddard also shifted away from this definition in attempting a more humanistic argument in support of America's restrictive immigration policy.

After the presentation of this definition, Stoddard then listed two factors that he did not feel to be particularly pertinent to the debate. First, he stated that the issue of the biological superiority or inferiority of the various European stocks would not fall within the consideration of the debate resolution. Although he admitted that such was a controversial issue, he claimed that a discussion of biological eugenicism would lead the discussion "far afield and into technicalities." This exclusion of an issue by Stoddard was important, because it served to benefit Darrow's overall position more than his own, in that it removed another possible avenue of advantage accrual to be gained by the people of the United States through restrictive immigration. Strategically, the exclusion of this issue worked to Stoddard's disadvantage.

Second, Stoddard excluded from consideration any argument concerning "the principle of numerical limitation of immigration," or quotas. The specified reason for this exclusion was that a discussion of quotas would tend to bog down the entire debate in useless numerical quibbling. Darrow consented to this exclusion, but then Stoddard, in his rebuttal presentation, completely contradicted his own exclusion by indicting Darrow for his failure to

Table V   Major Arguments in the Darrow-Stoddard Debate

Lothrop Stoddard	Clarence Darrow
Immigration policy should be concerned with the best interests of the American people	Potential immigrants deserve an opportunity for a better chance
Immigration restriction is needed for self-preservation —economic factors —social factors —political factors —racial factors	Restriction is injustice to immigrants —need people to settle the country —stemmed from mistaken patriotism —immigrants are not significantly different
Immigration restriction is in the best interests of foreigners to avoid the ill will of the American people	
Immigration restriction tries to maintain the proportion of the population	Immigration restriction interferes with the laws of nature

deal with the question of a quota system:

There was a delightfulness in the way in which he did not meet my very categorical questions of numerical restriction. I cannot tell you what he stands for or where he stands on that matter of numerical restriction, and that is the crux of the whole question underlying the immigration law . . . it is a matter of very vital concern to every American working man today, and it concerns his children, and his children's children. [28]

Not only did Stoddard completely reverse his initial position that quotas were unimportant to the consideration of the particular debate proposition, but by the rebuttal periods quotas had become the most important issue of the debate.

If a debater were allowed to exclude an issue from consideration in a debate and then indict his opponent for not dealing with that issue, obviously the initial debater would possess a massive strategic advantage. However, once an issue has been ruled out of consideration, it cannot be so easily reintroduced as Dr. Stoddard attempted to do. In short, Stoddard tried to pull an

unethical trick upon Darrow; however, the lack of subtlety therein made his attempt appear rather foolish.

After the presentation of the two issues that were supposedly excluded from consideration, Stoddard then moved to the recitation of his major lines of argumentation (see Table V). First, he claimed that the exclusion of southern European immigrants was justified in that such a policy furthered the preservation of the people and society of the United States. In the presentation of this argument, Stoddard utilized a four-part substructure in support of his assertion: economic, social, political, and racial. These parts of the argumentative substructure consumed most of his speaking time.

Stoddard justified immigration restriction economically by claiming that immigrants "came to this country with low living standards," and, as such, could be employed at lower wages than an American workingman. Because of this factor, Stoddard asserted immigration could destroy the American economy:

Everywhere you see protective measures taken by countries with high living standards *against countries with low living standards, and for that very reason it has become very much more imperative for us to keep our barriers, otherwise immigrants will come from all parts of the world by the tens of millions . . . . We shall be swamped economically . . . .*[29]

Therefore, immigration restriction was necessary to maintain the viability of the American workingman and the American economy. A liberal immigration policy, in Stoddard's view, would destroy the prosperity that characterized most of the 1920s in the United States.

Socially, Stoddard justified the 1924 immigration law in that it recognized the significant differences among cultural groups. Specifically, Stoddard claimed that the restrictive policy served to abort a potentially dangerous clash between such rival cultural practices:

These people from southern and eastern Europe had different habits, manners, customs, attitudes, and domestic relations between themselves and their neighbors and their community as a whole–a whole series of difficulties which inevitably made trouble both among themselves and between them and the Nordic element in the population.[30]

Assuming that cultural differences would inevitably lead to social confrontation and that such differences could never be reconciled, Stoddard argued that restrictive immigration was advantageous to the people of the United States in averting both intracultural and intercultural strife. This argument went hand in hand with the popular concern over the lack of "Americanization" of many of the immigrant groups and served as a point of refutation to the "melting pot" concept of the United States.

Stoddard then justified restrictive immigration upon political grounds, claiming that different governmental traditions in the Old World made them both uncomfortable with and unsuitable to the demands of democratic government in the United States:

These southern and eastern immigrants have different traditions. They do not accept democratic self-government and trial by jury . . . they have never known anything else but despotism–oppressive despotism. They have never been a real nationality. All the nationalities they have known were oppressive. Why should they have any concept of government and nationality in our sense?[31]

Thus, Stoddard feared that continued immigration of these "nondemocratic" peoples would bring eventual ruin to the democratic government of the United States. To protect American institutions, southern and eastern European immigrants must be prevented from coming to this country.

Finally, Stoddard concluded the substructure in support of the self-preservation line of argumentation by contending that racial differences between Nordics and other stocks were an important problem. The only way to deal with these differences was to allow the passage of time to reconcile them, and a highly restrictive immigration policy would provide this needed time. It should be noted that this final argument differed significantly from the preceding three arguments in that the factor of time was disadvantageous to the American people within the initial three arguments, but time was advantageous in the last argument, a most interesting shift in conception.

With his time almost expired, Stoddard quickly asserted two final arguments in support of restrictive immigration. First, he claimed that such a policy was advantageous to the southern and eastern Europeans in that exclusion prevented confrontation with the resentful majority within the United States.[32] Without such a restrictive policy, Stoddard claimed, there would be massive confrontations between immigrant and native groups, and the immigrants would suffer the most. Therefore, to avoid this situation, minimal immigration would allow the best of potential immigrants to enter the country without provoking this feared domestic upheaval. This argument provided a shift in emphasis from the operational definition of "advantage" provided by Stoddard earlier. Whereas he was initially concerned with the interests of the people of the United States as a whole, within this foregoing argument he was concerned with "the best interests of the southern and eastern [European] elements." Stoddard's decision to move toward a humanistic argument caused him to violate his own definition of terms that were to set the parameters of the debate. His own strategic maneuver caused him to shift definitions, another unethical change of position in midstream.

Second, Stoddard's final argument was that immigration restriction was justifiable upon the grounds that it served to maintain the internal proportions of the population:

It [the National Origins Quota System Plan] tries to maintain the proportion of our population as it now exists. And only by basing our immigration laws upon such a basis will our common good be assured.[33]

This last argument assumed the benefit of immigration control in claiming that maintenance of population proportions was a positive good. The argument, to have full impact and effect, was required to beg the question that immigration restriction was beneficial overall. Nonetheless, this final argument

served as an appropriate conclusion to a position that advocated minimal increase of immigration so as to maximize the benefits of maintaining a native Nordic population.

Clarence Darrow's Lines of Argumentation and Strategy

In speaking for the negative position, Clarence Darrow opted to utilize a point-by-point system of refutation that dealt with the specific arguments lodged by Lothrop Stoddard. Such an approach provided a very clear dichotomy between the major lines of argumentation and should have allowed the members of the audience to visualize the major differences in philosophy that were represented by the two debaters.

This philosophical difference was immediately demonstrated upon Darrow's direct response to Stoddard's definition of "advantage" within the debate resolution: "the interest of the people of the United States as a whole." Unlike this definition, Darrow's concern with advantageousness encompassed the concept that all potential immigrants to the United States deserved the opportunity to better themselves and their chances in life:

I can imagine myself being an Italian and wanting a better chance, or being a Russian Jew and wanting a better chance, or being an Austrian and wanting a better chance. It is hard for me to forget that there are other people on earth besides the stock I came from . . . . He speaks of the people in the United States as if they owned this country. Why, the first of them came over on the Mayflower. They couldn't stay at home without going to jail for debt . . . . They came over here to get a chance.[34]

Thus, Darrow's response to Stoddard's definition clearly indicated the difference in philosophy between the speakers: Stoddard was concerned with the welfare of the American people as a whole; Darrow was concerned with the availability of opportunity for all potential citizens to improve their lives. This philosophical split continued throughout the debate and presented the one major factor upon which the decision of the debate ultimately rested. As in all debates that deal with a resolution of value, the Darrow-Stoddard clash presented a dichotomy of philosophies upon which all of the disputed issues hinged. Audience members would tend to identify with one or the other major philosophies, and the remainder of the debate would be seen from this philosophical context. Thus, within ten minutes of the negative speaker's first presentation, the basis for decision had been tightly drawn for the members of the audience.

From this initial position of "opportunity for potential immigrants," Darrow moved to a consideration of the four-part "self-preservation" argument initiated by Stoddard, and his specific responses herein further clarified Darrow's humanistic philosophy. First, in a direct extension of his statement of philosophy, Darrow claimed that restrictive immigration policies perpetuated an injustice upon all immigrants:

I don't think justice can ever grow on injustice; I don't believe that kindness and humanity can ever come from selfishness. I do not believe that because we get to a place first we should say to others like ourselves, 'You can't come.'[35]

Therefore, Darrow claimed, we should institute a liberal immigration policy that was based upon a loving humanity and kindness, not a policy that stemmed from fear and selfishness. Such an argument grew

directly from the generalized humanism espoused earlier by Darrow.

In the rebuttal period, Stoddard responded to this argument by asserting that justice should begin at home, inferring that it was more important to do right by the American people before becoming concerned with the needs and wants of immigrants. This response was but a mere rewording of Stoddard's initial statement of philosophy and definition of terms, again demonstrating the philosophical difference between the men. These views were not reconciled throughout the debate, and they remained the central controversy of importance.

In dealing with Stoddard's specific argumentative substructure, Darrow issued three separate lines of refutation. First, concerning the putative social factors that rationalized restrictive immigration, Darrow argued that continued immigration was a societal necessity in settling and improving the country, claiming that the United States "isn't a quarter settled, nor a tenth."[36] Unlike the previous arguments, this piece of refutation rested upon a pragmatic approach, not one based upon philosophy. Darrow claimed that immigration was necessary to help develop the United States, an argument that strategically aimed at Stoddard's definition of advantage as anything that would be of benefit to the American people as a whole. Obviously, if the immigrant groups could aid in further settling the country, they could be, in fact, advantageous to everyone in the country.

As expected, Stoddard did not accept this argument; on the contrary, he directly refuted the evidential underpinning:

We hear that this country is only one-tenth settled, that there is plenty of room for everybody. As a matter of fact, those scientists who have investigated the problem have said that this country is already pretty well settled, and the general estimate is that there is room for 190,000,000 or 200,000,000 people in the United States . . . .[37]

Stoddard's response was the only argument within the debate that was based upon the presentation of factual evidence. All other arguments were either theoretical or philosophical in nature. However, neither debater extended his argument from this initial clash of supposed facts; both speakers merely reasserted their particular claims throughout the remainder of the debate.

Concerning Stoddard's argument that political differences rationalized restrictive immigration, Darrow retorted that such a rationale was based upon renegade patriotism:

. . . it [restrictive immigration] came from the mistaken idea of patriotism. This kind of patriotism is a heritage from the war; it was handed down by the army, the navy, and now it is being dispensed throughout Rotary Clubs, the Eagles, and other clubs that are shouting themselves hoarse about patriotism; they know nothing about it.[38]

Not only did this argument deal directly with Stoddard's political argument, it also tied in with the basic humanistic philosophy that characterized Darrow's overall position. Whereas Stoddard was seen to represent selfish, paranoid interests, Darrow chose to speak on a higher plane that emphasized kindness and charity, thus reinforcing the philosophical split between the debaters.

Darrow's final line of argumentation dealt with Stoddard's position that restrictive immigration was justified because of significant racial differences between southern and eastern European immigrants and the native Nordic Americans. Darrow flatly denied this difference, claiming instead that there existed no major dissimilarities between the racial stocks.[39] Therefore, upholding the "melting pot" concept in a *de facto* manner, Darrow charged that one race was as good as another, thereby denying the argument that racial considerations justified any sort of restrictive immigration policy.

Darrow vs. Stoddard: Evaluation

As has been stated several times throughout the presentation of Stoddard's and Darrow's respective arguments, the philosophical differences demonstrated by a consideration of a debate resolution of value actually controlled both the flow and the decision of the debate. Because the debaters visualized exceedingly different conceptions of what was an "advantage" to the United States and its people, there existed a great difficulty in dovetailing individual lines of argumentation. From the available information, it does appear that no audience vote was taken, at least there is no record of any such vote. Therefore, this writer did not possess any materials upon which to analyze and evaluate audience opinion. All that can be hypothesized is that the various audience members probably judged the debate upon the merits of the two major competing philosophies.

However, despite the absence of audience-oriented materials, an evaluation of the debate can be effectuated. First, it should be noted that there was a reasonably clear clash of ideas and issues throughout the constructive speeches of both debaters. Stoddard presented a well-organized case of arguments on behalf of his position, and Darrow responded directly to those arguments, maintaining the basic organization laid down by Stoddard. Unlike the debate with Will Durant, the issues were clear and the presentation of the arguments regarding those issues was similarly clear so as to maximize understanding. Thus, there was no question as to where each man stood concerning the debate topic, and there was no question as to the reasons supporting each man's position. The audience should have been able to perceive the argumentative differences between Darrow and Stoddard.

However, like the other four debates covered within this study, the rebuttal periods were, generally speaking, a forensic nightmare. Instead of extending the analysis initially developed within the constructive periods and basing such extensions upon the refutation offered by the opposition speaker, generally both debaters simply repeated their initial arguments. Because of this fact, the rebuttal periods mainly served to prolong the debate, rather than to aid in the further narrowing of the issues involved. This indictment must fall with particular weight upon Lothrop Stoddard, because he dropped the vast majority of his major arguments in rebuttal.

As noted previously, Stoddard's major line of argumentation centered upon the concept that restrictive immigration was necessary for the "self-preservation" of the United States and this position was supported by a four-part substructure. During rebuttals, Stoddard merely reiterated this general concept and entirely dropped the economic, social, political, and racial arguments that had served to substantiate the general claim. In addition, he failed to respond to two of Darrow's four main indictments of this contention, thereby placing himself in a strategically disadvantageous position.

Darrow, on the other hand, did not drop his four indictments of Stoddard's position. While his rebuttal arguments were nothing more than a repetition of constructive arguments, at least he did not allow the issues to fall by the wayside, taking advantage of Stoddard's strategic error. Thus, simply through the affirmative speaker's negligence, Darrow was able to cripple effectively the supportive substructure of Stoddard's major line of argumentation.

Surprisingly, Stoddard chose to dwell upon two relatively insignificant issues during rebuttals: restrictive immigration was advantageous to the excluded Europeans and such an immigration policy was beneficial in maintaining population proportions. Neither argument, separately or conjointly, was of sufficient weight to overwhelm Darrow's negative refutation. Whatever caused Stoddard to drop his strongest line of argumentation in favor of his weakest was not explained. However, this strategic decision was a grievous error in that it allowed Darrow to carry the most important arguments and, with them, the debate itself. Because of this error on the part of Stoddard, the negative refutation gained argumentative preeminence, and Clarence Darrow would be considered the victor in this particular confrontation.

One other strategic consideration should be noted. For an unspecified reason, Stoddard chose not to concern himself with the issue of supposed biological inferiority of southern and eastern European immigrants in support of a restrictive immigration policy. Because this was an area in which he possessed a great deal of knowledge and expertise, Stoddard could have immeasurably improved the qualitative strength of this overall argumentative case by introducing this issue. While it cannot be known how Darrow would have responded to this particular line of argumentation, the issue of biological inferiority certainly could not have done any further damage to Stoddard's position. Instead, it might have been the issue with which he could have salvaged the debate. Unfortunately for Dr. Stoddard, he did not introduce this issue, and the major arguments fell quite heavily to the negative speaker, Clarence Darrow.

Footnotes

[1] Frank L. Auerbach, ed., *Immigration Laws of the United States*, second edition (New York, 1961), p. 3.

[2] *Ibid.*, p. 5.

[3] Frederick Lewis Allen, *Only Yesterday* (New York, 1931), p. 14.

[4] Oscar Handlin, *The Uprooted* (Boston, 1951), p. 279.

[5] Paul L. Murphy, "Sources and Nature of Intolerance in the 1920s," *Journal of American History*, LI (June, 1964), p. 63.

[6] William Preston, Jr., *Aliens and Dissenters–Federal Suppression of Radicals, 1903-1933* (Cambridge, 1963), p. 4.

[7] *Ibid.*, pp. 240-241.

[8] The *New York Times*, December 4, 1924, p. 8.

[9] Wesley L. Jones, "Immigration," *The Congressional Digest*, II (July-August, 1923), p. 304.

[10] Don S. Kirschner, *City and Country–Rural Responses to Urbanization in the 1920s* (Westport, 1970), p. 28.

[11] Handlin, p. 278.

[12] Lothrop Stoddard, *The Rising Tide of Color* (New York, 1920), p. 162.

[13] An excellent examination of eugenic claims was made by Professor Joseph Gillman of the University of Pittsburgh with the resultant discovery that the statistical methods and procedures of the eugenicists were both invalid and unreliable. See Joseph Gillman, "Statistics and the Immigration Problem," *The American Journal of Sociology*, XXX (July, 1924), pp. 29-48.

[14] Auerbach, pp. 8-9.

[15] *Ibid.*, p. 472.

[16] Henry Pratt Fairchild, "The Immigration Law of 1924," *The Quarterly Journal of Economics*, XXXVIII (August, 1924), p. 665.

[17] Roderick Nash, *The Nervous Generation: American Thought, 1917-1930* (Chicago, 1970), p. 145.

[18] The *New York Times*, July 2, 1924, p. 18.

[19] Handlin, p. 295.

[20] The *New York Times*, October 17, 1924, p. 23.

[21] Arthur Garfield Hays, *Let Freedom Ring* (New York, 1928), p. x.

[22] Auerbach, p. 480.

[23] *The National Cyclopedia of American Biography*, 1955, LX, pp. 370-371.

[24] Lothrop Stoddard, *The Revolt Against Civilization* (New York, 1922), pp. 88-89.

[25] Stoddard, *The Rising Tide of Color*, p. 289.

[26] *Ibid.*, p. 165.

[27] Clarence Darrow and Lothrop Stoddard, *Is the U.S. Immigration Law Beneficial?* (Girard, 1929), p. 3.

[28] *Ibid.*, p. 16.

[29] *Ibid.*, pp. 18-19.

[30] *Ibid.*, p. 6.

[31] *Ibid.*, pp. 6-7.

[32] *Ibid.*, p. 8.

[33] *Ibid.*, p. 9.

[34] *Ibid.*, p. 10.

[35] *Ibid.*, p. 25.

[36] *Ibid.*, p. 13.

[37] *Ibid.*, p. 21.

[38] *Ibid.*, pp. 13-14.

[39] *Ibid.*, pp. 14-15.

Chapter Seven

Clarence Darrow: Analysis of the Public Advocate

Because of numerous pressures generated both by and with society, the decade of the 1920s was an era of immense turbulence in American history. These pressures came together to create a situation of massive societal dissonance, a situation in which large groups of people sought stability in an era of change and instability. The aftermath of the First World War saw a national hysteria over possible internal subversion and rebellion that caused an increase in social intolerance for minority views and opinions. Fear of Bolshevism and domestic radicalism led to the desire for "one-hundred-percent Americanism" and the restriction of foreign immigration. Lofty international ideals that had been espoused by Woodrow Wilson were shunned as America turned inward to take stock of her institutions and civilization.

At the same time, the United States underwent a rapid increase in urbanization and industrialization as the country moved from a rural society to an urban society that came to depend increasingly upon the magic of technology. As crop prices fell, farmers by the thousands abandoned their land to seek employment in the large metropolitan areas, and, for the first time, the majority of the American people lived in cities. Urban ghettos were created, crime dramatically increased, and the American people tried to make sense out of a rapidly changing social environment.

Since this societal dissonance created a national living condition that was intolerable to most Americans,

various avenues were explored to reduce dissonance by bringing stability to society. National policies of prohibition, highly restrictive immigration, and the increase of religious fundamentalism served as attempts at dissonance reduction. Prohibitionists perceived that many of the problems plaguing society sprang directly from the distillation and consumption of alcohol, and, therefore, they succeeded for a time in creating a national "dry" policy. However, Prohibition turned from being a liberal, progressive reform into a vindictive, reactionary policy, and the "noble experiment" failed after a thirteen-year trial period.

Restrictive immigration policies tried to exclude the alien element from American society, an element thought by many to be responsible for the worst of society's problems. Based upon the concept that certain groups of people were biologically superior to others, restrictive immigration attempted to create a uniquely American society by excluding those individuals and groups who did not conform to the norm. However, these policies created division rather than unity, and it was quickly discovered that societal problems continued to exist despite the exclusion of large numbers of potential immigrants.

For other individuals, a strict adherence to basic Biblical scripture served as a rallying point for social stability. As the national environment appeared to shift rapidly and threateningly, religious fundamentalists sought universal truths upon which to build their lives and the functions of society.

However, many persons came to discover that religious fundamentalism created more, instead of reducing, societal dissonance, because this religious practice did not mesh well with the contemporary shifts within society. Religious fundamentalism looked to the past for stability but was unable to provide the needed answers to those future questions posed by a rapidly changing society.

Thus, the era of the 1920s was one in which change and uncertainty stimulated various attempts at societal stabilization policies and practices. This was not an era of national frivolity and dissipation; this was not an era of wanton pleasure-seeking; this was not the era of "The Lost Generation" as depicted by novelists. On the contrary, the 1920s was a decade in which the majority of the American people were actively concerned with the great social issues of the day and with the dialogues that transpired upon those issues. Expansion of the mass media carried these great issues into the homes of Americans with greater frequency and depth than ever before, and national political and social leaders attempted to come to grips with these pressing issues in full view of the populace.

One of these social leaders was Clarence Darrow, famous criminal attorney from Chicago. His activities throughout the decade of the 1920s created national headlines that focused attention upon many of the important social issues of the time. In addition to his courtroom cases that dealt with highly significant matters, exemplified by his pronouncements upon criminology and capital punishment in the Loeb and Leopold trial and upon religious fundamentalism in the Scopes trial, Darrow also engaged in numerous public discussions upon the major social issues of the decade. This study examined five of Darrow's public debates upon the issues of capital punishment, Prohibition, the meaning of life itself, and upon restrictive immigration policy. From this examination and analysis, certain conclusions can be drawn that bear upon Darrow's career as a public advocate.

Quality of the Debates

All five debates examined within this study concentrated their discussion upon important issues of the 1920s. Capital punishment had been utilized as society's ultimate weapon against the criminal element that plagued that society, but an expansion of humanist doctrine, best exemplified by Darrow, and an increased concern with sociological and biological causes of crime created grave questions concerning the viability and effectiveness of the death penalty. Darrow engaged in a confrontation with Judge Alfred J. Talley over capital punishment in 1924, and this debate clearly presented the two major opposing views most prevalent during the 1920s and, to a large extent, the 1970s.

Public debates with John Haynes Holmes and Wayne Wheeler on national prohibition policy dramatized the importance of a national ban upon alcohol. Was Prohibition a positive attempt to uplift society or was it but another excuse to circumscribe individual freedom of action? Such a question appeared throughout Darrow's prohibition debates. It dealt with the heart of any national social policy and retains importance for society at any period during its development.

The public discussion with Will Durant upon the meaning of life and the functions of man clearly demonstrated the uncertainty of thought upon this issue existent during the 1920s and which probably continues into the present time. Does man have free will? Is man responsible for all his actions? Does man function as a divinely inspired, dynamic being, or is man nothing but a machine composed of flesh and blood? These questions were considered within the Darrow-Durant debate, and the inability of the debaters to present any viable conclusions indicated the complexity, as well as the crucial significance, of the questions asked.

Finally, Darrow's debate with Lothrop Stoddard upon the national policy of restrictive immigration concerned itself with more than a simple consideration of worldwide population flow. Were certain racial groups superior to others? Was American society unable to assimilate certain types of immigrant groups? Did the presence of Old World people pose a threat to the sanctity and prosperity of the American civilization? These questions went beyond forensic quibbling over arbitrary immigration quota systems; they dealt with the nature of American society and with the view that Americans had of their society. Similar questions were posed during the McCarthy era of the early 1950s and they shall certainly be posed again in the future whenever the structural makeup of society itself is brought into controversial examination.

Clarence Darrow's public debates during the 1920s focused upon such important social issues of the times. Because of the importance of these considerations to the national dialogue on such issues and to the career and philosophy of Darrow himself, these public debates merit greater consideration than they have received up to this time. Not only did these debates reveal a great deal about Darrow, they also revealed an important body of information about society itself and its concerns during

a crucial decade of the twentieth century.

A final comment upon the forensic quality of the debates must be added. From an academic forensic viewpoint, the five debates must be considered to be no more than mediocre in quality. More often than not, the debates became boring repetitions of arguments initially presented by the debaters involved; there was a general tendency to avoid argumentative extensions and specific refutations of an opponent's line of thought. There was a universal lack of direct clash with one another's major lines of argumentation, thereby creating more heat than light in dealing with a highly controversial subject. Evaluations of each individual debate were similar in that they all reflected an inability to make rebuttal periods worthwhile either to the audience or to the debaters themselves. Darrow's confrontation with Will Durant clearly demonstrated the dangers inherent in a debate between two people who speak upon two different issues under one general topic, and, because of this problem, this debate was of the poorest quality of the five studied. On the other hand, Darrow's debate with Judge Talley demonstrated a direct clash of ideas upon the same issues, thereby creating a crisp confrontation of views and opinions; this debate was highest in quality of the five debates studied.

While it was probably true that the audiences for these debates came with rigidly fixed predispositions toward the issues under consideration,[1] the intrinsic quality of the debates could have been improved immensely by the utilization of direct clash procedures by the debate chairman, thereby forcing the debaters to deal with the same issues upon the same terms. The failure to employ such procedures created a lack of argumentative relevance as the debater often spoke of issues and ideas irrelevant both to the topic in question and to the position of one's opponent. This failure lowered the quality of the debates and often created more confusion than clarity—the antithesis of the purpose of debate.

Clarence Darrow's Forensic Qualities

From the materials examined within this study, several conclusions can be drawn concerning Clarence Darrow's overall qualities as a public debater. While this study did not consider Darrow's courtroom speaking *per se*, the conclusions posed herein generally dovetail with many of the published and unpublished materials pertinent to his legal career. Three major forensic strengths have been noted. First, Darrow's presentation of material was exceptionally clear in the style of language employed. Darrow wrote in his autobiography that he constantly tried to "make my statements clear and simple and the sentences short."[2] Insofar as the debates examined within this study are concerned, Darrow succeeded in achieving his goal. There was absolutely no question as to what Darrow was saying or where he stood in relation to the issues under consideration. His easy conversational mode of speaking created an impression of good-natured friendliness and a "just plain folks" style that provided a marked contrast with his opponents, a contrast easily noted within the Darrow-Durant debate. Even if one disagreed with Darrow, the debate would be easy and pleasant to listen to, and if Darrow succeeded in this respect, then he had a chance of winning one over with his humanistic philosophy.

Second, another of Darrow's strengths was his utilization of humor throughout the debates analyzed. Not only was this humor of the knee-slapping variety, it also contained a large amount of concealed invective and sarcasm that could be devastating to the opponent's position. In 1927, David Lilienthal reported on Darrow's debate activity and concluded that his opponents "were routed not so much by Darrow's intellect as by his irresistible flow of good-natured cynicism."[3] Such a persistent utilization of humorous devices was particularly apparent within the Darrow-Talley debate, where Judge Talley dropped most of his important arguments under the caustic fire of Darrow's humor. One need only examine Darrow's sarcastic remarks about prosecuting attorney Savage in the Loeb-Leopold trial to perceive the carry-over from the courtroom to the debate circuit of this most effective forensic device.

Third, Darrow's forensic positions were strengthened by his general philosophical consistency throughout his career and his argumentative consistency in the various forms of public discourse. Although Darrow did not present any sort of "program" that he wished to implement to save mankind and society, he was philosophically consistent in his espousal of humanism. This consistency must be considered a strength in that it allowed Darrow to perceive many diverse and complex problems from the same context, thereby minimizing dissonance within his own cognition. Because of this consistency, Darrow tended to argue and to create lines of argumentation along consistently similar lines of thought and development. Jackson has noted that, in his forensic speaking, Darrow tended to utilize a four-step progression of argument: use of a backdrop of history, labelling one's opponent as a tool of some evil force, use of invective against the opponent, and the insistence that one's own position was based upon kindliness and other respectable qualities.[4] Every speech within the debates studied demonstrated that Darrow employed this four-step development in his public debating activities. Thus, Darrow had only to insert the particular arguments relevant to the issue under consideration into this overall four-step organizational pattern, creating an approach that maximized the ease with which Darrow could prepare himself for debate.

However, along with these strengths, Darrow also possessed certain weaknesses that detracted from his forensic effectiveness. In relation to the strength of argumentative consistency, Darrow exhibited a concomitant weakness in the internal development and organization of particular arguments. He tended to leave arguments dangling without bringing them to a close, to move on to another argument, and then abruptly to return to the first argument with no apparent reason for such jackrabbit movement. While he did employ the four-step development noted previously, these steps occurred randomly and in no particular sequence. This habit of disorganization was most apparent in the Darrow-Durant debate as arguments appeared and then disappeared at random, creating a debate that confused an already obfuscated topic, thereby negating the rationale for public debate.

A second weakness was Darrow's generally ineffective style of refutation. Time and again, he attempted to negate the position of his opponent by humorous invective and the issuance of bland rhetorical questions to the audience. Although it was true that most of his opponents withdrew from combat because of his effective use of humor, one could rightly expect to hear an in-depth discussion of significant issues that would be based upon the logical presentation of data and facts, not upon the utilization of witticisms that amused but did not enlighten. Darrow caused Judge Talley and Wayne Wheeler to drop important arguments through the effectiveness of his humor—an important forensic skill, but one that did not improve the national consciousness of the issues under discussion. Darrow's humor did not openly affect Will Durant, and for that reason, Darrow appeared to be the inferior debater.

The final major weakness of Darrow's debating as noted by this writer was his constant interjection of peripheral and irrelevant issues into the various debates. In every one of the five debates he spoke of burning witches in puritanical New England, although only two of the debates possessed material relevant to such a consideration. In the debate with Stoddard on immigration policy, Darrow launched a lengthy indictment of the American free enterprise system that, at best, served to cloud the important issue of the rights of immigrant labor. Those two examples demonstrated that Darrow's lack of a clear internal organization of materials caused him to wander far afield in the presentation of his argumentative case structure. The impact of this interjection of peripheral and irrelevant material was that the total force of Darrow's particular position was significantly decreased; solid refutation by his opponents could have placed Darrow in the disadvantageous position of being constantly on the defensive. However, only Will Durant took advantage of Darrow's weakness in this respect and it was for this prime reason that Durant was able to secure preeminence in their encounter.

Therefore, in final evaluation of Darrow's forensic capabilities,

Darrow must be considered an interesting, humorous public advocate whose style served often to detract from the strength of the arguments he offered. While his sarcastic wit and cynicism made him a worthy debate adversary, he certainly was not an invincible forensic speaker. An opponent who would present a well-organized and reasoned case, who would retain that organization and basic line of argumentation, and who would be willing to offer meaningful refutational arguments would cause Darrow to pale in comparison. John B. Watson, chairman of the Darrow-Durant debate, said that Darrow was "the world's most terrible speaker—terrible, that is, to the man who has to answer him."[5] Because of the nature of Darrow's debate weaknesses, Watson's analysis was more laudatory than accurate. Clarence Darrow was a man to contend with, but not to fear, in public debate.

Footnotes

[1] Abe C. Ravitz, *Clarence Darrow and the American Literary Tradition* (Cleveland, 1962), pp. 129-130.

[2] Clarence Darrow, *The Story of My Life* (New York, 1932), p. 381.

[3] David E. Lilienthal, "Clarence Darrow," *The Nation*, CXXIV (April 20, 1927), p. 418.

[4] James H. Jackson, "Clarence Darrow's Plea in Defense of Himself," *Western Speech*, XX (Fall, 1956), pp. 191-192.

[5] Clarence Darrow and Will Durant, *Are We Machines?* (Girard, 1928), p. 32.

Appendix One

Excerpts from the Darrow-Talley Debate

Judge Alfred J. Talley:

Now, there isn't much difficulty in defining the terms of this debate. "Is Capital Punishment a Wise Public Policy?" There can't be any misunderstanding as to precisely the purport of this discussion.

A wise policy is that which is reasonably calculated to accomplish the end which is sought. And in a country, such as ours, that policy should have the approval of the majority of the people of a republic. And capital punishment is the right exercised by the state to put to death one who has violated that law of the state which says, "Thou shalt not kill," and for a murder deliberated and premeditated upon, that penalty shall be imposed . . . .

In the heart of every man is written the law, "Thou shalt not kill." Upon the statute books of every civilized community is written the law, "Thou shalt not kill." And no one offends that precept through ignorance. It is fundamental that every man knows it is wrong and illegal to take the life of another man . . . .

Those who would abolish capital punishment would give this notice to the potential murderer: "You who have snatched away the life of one who had a right to live, you shall be tried by a jury of your peers. The state will see to it that you are defended by able counsel if you are without means to employ one for yourself. And if it should happen that a jury should determine that you are guilty of premeditative murder, you are then by reason of that verdict convicted of that crime, you shall not forfeit your life in return for the one which you destroyed, but you shall be incarcerated in a prison possibly—only possibly—for the remainder of your life. And when you are sent to that prison you shall be put into a cell, into which the sunlight of which you have deprived your victim must ever come. You shall be given some light labor for a few hours a day—fewer than ever falls to the lot of the average man who must earn his bread by the sweat of his brow amongst law-abiding, nonkilling people of the community. And you are given this labor not for what it might produce, but primarily that your time might be profitably to yourself employed. And you shall be given entertainment. If you happen to kill in the State of New York, you be provided with a moving picture show every night of the week, and at various times during the season prominent Broadway stars will bring up their companies and their paraphernalia for your entertainment. Your less fortunate brother, who has respected the law, must pay for that entertainment in the theatres of Broadway. But you, a ward of the state, will be provided with these without the necessity of paying for them at all. And you shall be given three meals a day—meals that will be supervised by a dietician employed by the State . . . .

The object of punishment of crime must be deterrent, and it must be vindictive—not vindictive in the sense of revengeful, but it must be imposed so that the law and its majesty and sanctity may be vindicated . . . .

I say that out of my own experience, as lawyer for defendant, as prosecutor for the state and as judge of the greatest criminal court in all the world, I say that the only thing the criminal fears is the penalty of death that will follow his crime. And I need not read that in any book or any essay or any treatise. That is my experience of more than twenty-five years . . . .

I say it is the time for sensible men and women to come to a realization that there is one way to deal with the criminal and the malefactor, and that is with certainty and severity. There is no other way in which the integrity of the people of this country or the sanctity of the law may be observed. I am in favor of abolishing capital punishment when the murderers of the country abolish its necessity.

Clarence Darrow:

I deny his statement that every man's heart tells him it is wrong to kill. I think every man's heart desires killing. Personally, I never killed anybody that I know of. But I have had a great deal of satisfaction now and then reading obituary notices, and I used to delight, with the rest of my hundred percent patriotic friends, when I saw ten or fifteen thousand Germans being killed a day.

Everybody loves killing. Some of them think it is too messy for them. Every human being that believes in capital punishment loves killing, and the only reason they believe in capital punishment is because they get a kick out of it. Nobody kills anyone for love, unless they get over it temporarily or otherwise. But they kill the one they hate. And before you can get a trial to hang somebody or electrocute him, you must first hate him and then get a satisfaction over his death . . . .

I might just observe, in passing, that in all of these states where the mortality by homicide is great, they have capital punishment and always have had it. A logical man, when he found out that the death rate increased upon capital punishment, would suggest some other way of dealing with it . . . .

We teach people to kill, and the state is the one that teaches them. If a state wishes that its citizens respect human life, then the state should stop killing. It can be done in no other way, and it will perhaps not be fully done that way. There are infinite reasons for killing. There are infinite circumstances under which there are more or less deaths. It never did depend and never can depend upon the severity of the punishment . . . .

If you want to get rid of killings by hanging people or electrocuting them because these are so terrible, why not make a punishment that is terrible? This isn't so much. It lasts but a short time. There is no physical torture in it. Why not boil them in oil, as they used to do? Why

not burn them at the stake? Why not sew them into a bag with serpents and throw them out to sea? Why not take them out on the sand and let them be eaten by ants? Why not break every bone in their body on the rack, as has been done for such serious offenses as heresy and witchcraft?

Why, our capital punishment isn't worth talking about, so far as its being a preventive is concerned. It isn't worth discussing. Why not call back from the dead and barbarous past the hundred and sixty or seventy odd crimes that were punishable by death in England? Why not once more reenact the Blue Laws of our own country and kill people right? Why not resort to all the tortures that the world has always resorted to to keep men in the straight and narrow path? Why reduce it to a paltry question of murder?

Let me take another statement of my friend. He said, "Oh, we don't hang anybody if they kill when they are angry; it is only when they act premeditatedly." Yes, I have been in courts and heard judges instruct people on this premeditated act. It is only when they act under their judgment and with due consideration. He would also say that if a man is moved by anger, but if he doesn't strike the deadly blow until such time as a reason and judgment has a chance to possess him, even if it is a second—how many times have I heard judges say, "Even if it is a second?" What does any judge know about premeditation? What does anybody know about it? How many people are there in this world that can premeditate on anything? I will strike out the "pre" and say how many people are there that can meditate?

But what is punishment about anyway? I put a man in prison for the purpose of getting rid of him and for such example as there might be. Is it up to you to torture him while he is there? Supposing you provided that every man who went to prison should be compelled to wear a nail half an inch long in his shoe. I suppose some of you would do it. I don't know whether the judge would or not, from what he said.

Is there any reason for torturing someone who happens to be in prison? Is there any reason why an actor or even an actress might not go there and sing? There is no objection to a preacher going there. Why not give him a little pleasure?

And they really get food there—what do you know about that? Now, when I heard him tell about what wonderful food they get—dietary food—did you ever know anybody that liked dietary food? I suppose the Constitution of the State of New York contains the ordinary provision against cruel and inhumane punishment, and yet you send them up there and feed them on dietary food . . . .

I never saw a man who wanted to go to prison, even to see the movies. I never saw a man in my life who didn't want to get out . . . .

All people are products of two things, and two things only—their heredity and their environment. And they act in exact accord with the heredity which they took from all the past, and for which they are in no way responsible, and the environment, which reaches out to the farthest limit of all life that can influence them. We all act from the same way. And it ought to teach us to be charitable and kindly and understanding.

Appendix Two

Excerpts from the Darrow-Holmes Debate

Dr. John Haynes Holmes:

All the strength that I can get as I enter upon the discussion of this question comes from my sincere conviction that there is justice in my cause. Consequently, I launch out upon the discussion of prohibition with the sentiment so well laid down by William Shakespeare in the last act of *Macbeth*. "Lay on McDuff, and damned be he who first cries hold, enough."

. . . we are discussing the policy of prohibition from the standpoint of the Eighteenth Amendment to the Constitution, and not from the standpoint of the Volstead Act. I am ready to assume, from the very drop of a hat, that the Volstead Act is unwise and ineffective and is not a success. I shall simply decline to discuss at all the policy of enforcement under the Volstead Act, but shall confine everything that I have to say this afternoon to the Eighteenth Amendment to the Constitution as a policy which should be continued by one form of legislation or another into the future . . . .

Talk about the Eighteenth Amendment constituting "a radical and revolutionary change in policy!" The Eighteenth Amendment came in the process of inevitable social development. It was the final fulfillment of a policy to which the overwhelming majority of the American people had long since dedicated themselves by the processes of democratic franchise and democratic legislation. It is that thing that I am talking about . . . .

. . . Laws are necessary for the life and happiness of society; that where many people are living together in one place and conducting the proceedings of a common life, the business of these many people must be conducted upon the basis of legislation, of agreements as to the program of the life they live together . . . .

You say, "Why has the state any right to dictate to me what I shall drink?" The state hasn't any right to dictate to you what you shall drink, provided that what you drink affects yourself alone and does not affect society at large. If any man should say to me or prove to me upon the basis of social experience and laboratory experiments that legislation against coffee does to society what the drinking of a glass of whiskey does, then I should say that legislation against coffee, like legislation against whiskey, was justified by the fact that the safety and happiness of us all must be protected from the invasion of the one or the two . . . .

Liquor in the first place is dangerous to the public safety. If it is necessary to have a locomotive driver sober, what about an automobile driver? We are living in the automobile age. Great automobiles are driven at rapid speeds through the streets of our cities and the highways of our country. Do you think it is compatible with public safety to allow the driver of an automobile, under any circumstances, to get liquor? Not at all! We have got to do what we can (however ineffectively) to relieve and save society from that kind of a menace.

Liquor is dangerous to public safety because it creates poverty, it cultivates crime, it establishes social conditions generally which are a burden to society.

Secondly, liquor legislation is social legislation because liquor constitutes a deliberate exploitation of the weak by the strong. The real thing that the Eighteenth Amendment was after—the real thing—was the liquor business, the manufacturing of liquor, the distribution of liquor, the sale of liquor under a public license—a business in the hands of a few for the amassing of great millions which preyed upon the weaknesses of the people if he were allowed to do so in the absence of tenement house legislation.

For these two reasons—because liquor is a menace to public safety, and an exploitation of the weak—we have got to get rid of it. And if you can show me any way of doing that thing apart from doing what we did to the slave trade, to chattel slavery, to the white slave traffic, to the opium trade, I would like to know what it is.

Clarence Darrow:

This is a question of the philosophy of government. And when I saw the kind of literature my friend reads, I knew that everything was going to be all right.

I am one of those, I will admit, in starting, whom he has more or less defined as doubtful and suspicious of authority. I don't like it. I think the less we have, the better. He describes that as bordering on the philosophical anarchist view. I would speak for that as against the extreme socialist view, which says that everything on earth should be regulated or controlled. Society is always moving between those two views. And, as a practical matter, neither one is correct. Society will never submit to an organization, in my opinion, where there is no authority of any sort by one man or another or by collective organization over others, and it will never, for long, submit to what is still more intolerable, the complete enslavement of the unit by the mass . . . .

I object to a man being drunk if he gets in the way of anybody else. I don't mind his being drunk alone. But if I want to take a drink and do not get drunk where I interfere with anybody else, should society then tell me that I can't drink? Or, if Brother Holmes—no I will not use him; I will take the Chairman—if he hasn't got any more sense than to get drunk, is that any reason why I, who do not get drunk, shall not have anything to drink? Now—is it?

I say that nobody in their right senses would trust their individual liberty to the people who believe in that sort of legislation . . . .

I don't believe in the Eighteenth Amendment, but it is here. And I wouldn't believe in it if I knew that the people in this country could get richer under it; I still don't believe in it. Of course, they would get richer without coffee, in which he seems to believe, and

he probably drinks it. Everybody believes in what they want and they are not interested in what the other fellow wants, unless they want it too.

It isn't a question simply whether prohibition would be good if there ever was any such thing. Of course, we don't know whether it would be good or not, yet. I never knew anybody with money who couldn't get a drink. Do any of you? I would agree to find places here, although I am a stranger. I wouldn't have to look far. They would come to me. I never knew anybody in this land of ours, under the Amendment and under the Volstead Act, to go thirsty.

Of course, it has raised the price. It hasn't placed it within the reach of all. It has substituted whiskey for beer to many people—which I think is a poor substitution. It has made people drink gin and whiskey where they once chose wine—which is a poor substitution. It has done all of those things. And I imagine there is no system of prohibition under which it will not always do those things, and that is practically the only thing it will do.

Now, suppose we admit, for the sake of argument, that sixty percent of the people of this country would vote dry. If sixty percent of the people do not believe in something that the other forty percent believe in, should they send the forty percent to jail for what they do?

Now, there is your question. What proportion of a population should believe that certain acts are criminal before passing a criminal statute? If forty percent of the people of this country believe that a thing is innocent, do you think that the sixty percent who do not believe it would send that forty percent to jail if they were tolerant people?

I assume that sixty percent of the people in this country believe in either the Protestant or Catholic religion, or think they do, and believe that it is very necessary to man's welfare on earth and absolutely necessary to his welfare in the hereafter. Are they justified in passing a criminal statute and sending heretics to jail?

The prohibitionist is the lineal descendant of the Puritan. I didn't know it before, but even my friend here says that he came from Massachusetts. But he believes somewhat in freedom. He believes in the liberty of speech and of the press. Well, there are some people that like to do something besides talking and writing. That doesn't cover the whole range of liberty. Almost every sort of conduct has been hedged around in this world by fanatics . . . .

This prohibition law has filled our jails with people who are not criminals, who have no conception or feeling that they are doing wrong. It has turned our federal courts into police courts, where important business is put aside for cases of drunkardness and disorderly conduct. It has made spies and detectives, snooping around doors and windows. It has made informers of thousands of us. It has made grafters and boodlers of men who otherwise would be honest. It is hateful, it is distasteful, it is an abomination, and we ought to get rid of it, and we will if we have the courage and the sense.

Appendix Three

Excerpts from the Darrow-Wheeler Debate

Clarence Darrow:

I presume that even the prohibitionist would have meant that if a man is to live in this world he ought to have some freedom. There ought to be some things he could choose for himself. Instead of setting everybody to govern everybody else, each man ought to have something to do with the job of controlling himself. And if he has any liberty whatever it seems to me he ought to have a right to say what he should eat and what he should drink!

The world has seen men and women without number executed for witchcraft due to the zeal and bigotry of religious leaders. These executions have run over a period of four or five years. Even in America, supposed to be free, we have had examples of the hanging of old women for witchcraft in New England, a crime which all fairly intelligent people know today is an impossible crime. Of course, all women couldn't be guilty of witchcraft. Young ones might. But even with them it should not be a criminal offense. These same people have loaded the statutes of every state with Sunday observance laws, and in the City of New York today is an organization devoted to hunting up the people who have any pleasure on Sunday and passing a law to make it a crime.

After a while they will look around for babies who laugh on Sunday and try to have a law to stick pins into them because it is wicked to laugh on Sunday . . . .

Personally I have never yet noticed any drought. And I never expect to. All that has been accomplished is to take beer and wine away from people who can't afford the high prices. That is all. But they are getting around that. They are buying grape juice and letting the Lord make the wine for them. And the amount of grapes, running into ten or twelve times as much and increasing every year,

shows that there is hope even in spite of prohibition . . . .

It has never been enforced. It can never be enforced! Until the last spark of independence has fled from the heart of the American people they will never consent that an organized body of men shall tell them what they may drink and what they may not drink. There were human beings in the witchcraft days of New England and juries refused to convict until the law was dead. There are jurors today who have too much manhood to sit upon a jury and convict a fellow man for doing exactly what he has done and is doing! Where is the man in the United States today who doesn't drink or want to? And if he wants to badly enough he does. Juries refuse to convict for doing what they have done, and there are even judges who refuse to fine and imprison for doing what they habitually do!

Mr. Wayne B. Wheeler:

Intoxicating beverages have generally been admitted to be harmful to their users and to society. Intoxicating liquor contains alcohol, a narcotic, habit-forming drug or poison of which one can drink five ounces at once and live. Who are injured by this prohibition of the traffic in this recognized evil? Those who do not drink intoxicating liquor are not injured by such prohibition. Those who drink to excess and injure others dependent on them for support are not injured but benefitted, as are their dependents also. Those who drink enough to undermine their health or decrease their wealth-producing power will not be injured . . . .

The beverage liquor traffic has never had the standing in decent society which Mr. Darrow has unsuccessfully tried to give it for years. Booze was a social and moral outcast before the Eighteenth Amendment. Its best friends have always been apologetic about it. It was not named by its right names but given fine-sounding titles. It was King Alcohol—a name well chosen because he was the enemy to all that democracy stands for. All that poetry of language or that beauty of color could do was done to mask his real character, but under the fine names and the 'color that moveth itself aright in the cup' there was booze.

Booze undermined the national health through a century until 13.9 persons out of each 1,000 died yearly. Over 200,000 of these deaths were needless. When booze was banished, with its plague-laden breath, the death rate dropped and 200,000 fewer graves were dug per year. Masquerading as medicine, hiding its wolf's fangs under sheep's clothing, booze hurried the tubercular or the pneumonia patient to the grave while he pretended to give them new life. Its death roll surpasses that of the War God . . . .

No defender of beverage intoxicants can produce a single statement by a court of last resort declaring the liquor habit or traffic a good thing for the individual or for society, but thousands of decisions agree in declaring it so vicious, corrupting, pauperizing, health-destroying that it stands in a unique position before the courts and the nation . . . .

Good results have come in spite of the organized resistance to the enforcement of prohibition. Public drunkenness is rare; drink-caused crime has been greatly reduced; drink-caused poverty no longer drains millions in charity; alcoholism and alcoholic insanity are far below the license year average; drink no longer publicly tempts the weak but has become furtive; industrial accidents are fewer, the billions that once brought delirium tremens, crime, and poverty, now purchase homes, autos, insurance, travel, education, wholesome entertainment, bonds and stocks, with self-respect and happiness.

Appendix Four

Excerpts from the Darrow-Durant Debate

Dr. Will Durant:

It was the Industrial Revolution that filled the world with the strange notion that man is a machine. For first of all it accustomed the mind to dealing with machines and induces it more and more to think of causes not as biological, but as mechanical. The worker within the factory wall, seeing the busy activity slip about him on pulleys and revolve on wheels, forgot that older existence in which life had seemed to be a matter of seeds spontaneously sprouting from the soil, responding eagerly to every encouragement, and multiplying with an astounding and bountiful fertility. The world, which had once been a picture of growing plants and willful children, of loving mothers and ambitious men, became for the modern mind a vast array of mechanisms, from the planets that circled mechanically around the sun to the crowds that flocked mechanically to be in at the death of a moving-picture star. Science was sure now that it had at last been admitted behind the curtains of the cosmic drama. It marveled at the unsuspected machinery which had shifted a thousand scenes and created a million delusions. It concluded in modest admiration that the property man was the real dramatist and that the wires were the play . . . .

It may comfort you to know that at the moment when the theory of mechanism has reached down into popular favor, it is being abandoned in a great many of the sciences, in biology (not in psychology), in physiology, even in physics itself. Lucien Poincaré, one of the leading scientists of France, writes revealingly: "Today," he says, "the idea that all phenomena are capable of mechanical explanation is generally abandoned." The German scientist Cassiver says: "In modern physics the mechanical view of the world has been more and more superseded by the dynamic view." Le

Bon, one of the founders of the atomic physics, writes, "In spite of the efforts of thousands of workers, physiology has been able to tell us nothing of the nature of the forces that produce the phenomena of life. They have no analogy with those that are studied in physics."

Yet, don't imagine for a moment that I wish to rest my case on authorities. Let us do our own thinking and face the phenomena directly for ourselves. Let us observe the unmechanical spontaneity, and purposiveness and selectiveness of life . . . .

Let us in conclusion consider genius. Here is the creative power of life in its clearest and highest form. Here is the last product of that glorious vitality which dances in the atom and fills the soil and the sea and the air with living and growing things. Here is genius, mind turns around and remoulds the environment in which it grew. Man, the supposed machine, invents and operates machines, and craves beauty, and seeks truth, and creates social order, and rises to the loftiest reaches of morality and love. And I am asked to believe that the philosophic frenzy of Plato, the fine passion of Beethoven or Shakespeare, the divine intoxication of Spinoza, the godlike grandeur of Leonardo da Vinci's mind are mechanical processes, that the thoughts and the aspirations of these men were put into them with some mysterious time attachment by that mythical nebula a million millenia ago!

Well, I refuse to believe it. I cannot understand how any cautious and skeptical mind can so far forget itself as to accept so ridiculous a fairy story; and I wonder does Mr. Darrow realize how much credulity lies behind his unbelief, how much simple faith in untested and fallible authority? I do not believe that Chicago's leading citizen is a machine mechanically meditating upon its own machinery, an automaton automatically reflecting upon its own automatism. If I could believe that I could accept every fairy story ever told and every legend in every Bible ever written. After escaping from the infallibility of a church and from the infallibility of a physicist who tries to squeeze into his test tubes and his narrow formulae all this budding and teeming world, it is time we should put an end to this new age of faith, and come to doubt even our scientists when they speak to us of miracles in terms of a childish mythology.

Clarence Darrow:

My friend over here has been talking for forty minutes telling us what life is not, but not uttering a single word as to what it is. He has in the last analysis quoted Walt Whitman as the champion scientist of the world. Now, I read Walt Whitman when I don't care to think but just want to feel, and when he says that "Holiness is life," it reminds me of Mary Baker Eddy when she said, "God is love and love is God." No use of having two words for the same thing. Is holiness life? Bunk! It may sound good, but it has nothing whatever to do with the subject . . . .

What I do contend is this: That the manifestation of the human machine and of living organisms is very like unto what we know as a machine, and that if we could find it all out we would probably find that everything had a mechanistic origin . . . .

What do we know about the human machine? We know that it takes one form of energy and transposes it into another. We know that we give it food which in the human system is broken up and the energy that results is transferred into something else. Let us look at the process that the human machine goes through in this transformation of energy and see whether it resembles any other machine, and if it doesn't, then what? Is there some mysterious thing about man which for lack of some other word, or for lack of any word that any human being can understand, we call a soul? Does he stand out here separated from nature, and stand alone? Let us see what man does.

We feed him, or he can't live and he can't work. We place food in his mouth. What happens to it? It is digested. The energy in the food is released and goes into the body just exactly the same as the energy placed in the coal box of an engine is released and makes steam. How does it go? It is first taken care of by certain juices and is digested. It passes into the intestine. Then what happens? This digested food is power, just like the coal; it is energy. If a man is to work, if the body is to live, this energy must become a part of him. It must go to his brain, if he has any, to his feet, to every part of him. How does it get there? Man has a circulatory system made of arteries and blood vessels. The artery at the intestine is separated by only a very small lining from the intestines. The juices of the intestine pass into the blood, some of the blood to the intestines. As it goes by these juices are absorbed; this food is absorbed; this energy is absorbed; the power is absorbed—a simple, plain obviously mechanical process . . . .

I don't say I am sure that there is nothing in man but a mechanism in the same sense that I am sure that two and two make four. There are a very few things in the world of which I am as sure as that, and I am not sure of that. It would depend upon what the two things and the other things were, perhaps, before I'd be sure they would make four. Two philosophers and two religionists wouldn't make four anything. They'd make two philosophers and two religionists. That's all.

I am sure of it to a mathematical demonstration. But I am fairly sure of enough things which to me warrant the inference that when the story is all told, if it ever is told, this will be the conclusion.

Appendix Five

Excerpts from the Darrow-Stoddard Debate

Dr. Lothrop Stoddard:

I shall not include in my argument any discussion of the principle of numerical limitation of immigration. Both Mr. Darrow and myself will keep away from the issue of absolute numbers. There should be some numerical limit, however the various racial quotas are to be laid down as a matter of public law in this country. Most thinking people in this country believe that to open our gates wide to immigration would be to destroy our precious prosperity, to depress our wage standard, to upset our whole economic life, not to speak of our political and national life, and no one appreciates those things better than labor. You know the decisive step taken by the American Federation of Labor at New Orleans recently when they came out for restriction of immigration because it is labor which has the most to gain from keeping standards high by allowing only a few wage-earners to enter this country. They know what happened in past years, before the immigration law of 1924, when from one million to one million and a half people came into this country in one year, putting our whole industrial system upon a hire and fire basis . . . .

First let us look at the economic factors of this situation, for that was really the first and foremost factor. Comparatively few of the people who supported the immigration law of 1924 were actuated solely by race feeling. This question was touching their pocketbooks, their wages. It was touching them economically in numerous ways. The great majority of immigrants from southern and eastern Europe were from the poorest classes of a poor and backward race. They came to this country with low living standards, and they came with strange business and social customs which produced a very

serious and a very aggravating and annoying disturbance in the economic life of the country . . . .

These people from southern and eastern Europe had different habits, manners, customs, attitudes, and domestic relations between themselves and their neighbors and their community as a whole—a whole series of difficulties which inevitably made trouble both among themselves and between them and the Nordic element in the population . . . .

I must not dodge the unfortunate results of this immigration law. I will freely admit that some of the results have been unfortunate. It has undoubtedly caused a great deal of ill feeling. It has hurt the feelings of the southern Europeans in this country. But why look exclusively at that side of the picture? What about the feelings of the older stocks? Consider the vast majority of the nation. These southern people number fourteen or fifteen percent of our population. How about the feelings of the great majority, who have been thoroughly aroused, thoroughly alarmed, and thoroughly determined that something must be done to preserve their country as I have stated? If their feelings are disregarded, will there not be a great amount of feeling and unrest produced? And from the standpoint of the southern European, will it not be to their best interests to avoid the ill will and the bitter feeling of the majority? The only way out is to adhere to the National Origins Plan, a plan which will give proper importance to all the immigrants in this country at the present time, and to their descendants. It provides a larger proportion for the races of southern Europe than does the census of 1890. It tries to maintain the proportion of our population as it now exists. And only by basing our immigration laws upon such a basis will our common good be assured.

Clarence Darrow:

The law as it stands today, passed in 1924, provides that 150,000 immigrants may come to the United States annually, and that the number should be fixed for each country according to the number of citizens of that country who had emigrated to the United States, but that it should be the number of citizens who had emigrated previous to 1890—thirty-five years before the law was passed. Instead of using 1924 as the basis of immigration quotas, they dated it back thirty-five years. Why? So they could get Nordics from England and Scotland, and Norway, and Sweden, and exclude the people from Italy, France, and the Balkan states, and Russian Jews . . . .

Our friend talks about the right of countries to do things. Countries have rights only when they have power to enforce them. I don't agree with him because I have imagination; that is all. I can imagine myself being an Italian and wanting a better chance, or being a Russian Jew and wanting a better chance, or being an Austrian and wanting a better chance. It is hard for me to forget that there are other people on earth besides the stock I came from.

He speaks of the people in the United States now as if they owned this country. Why, the first of them came over on the Mayflower. They couldn't stay at home without going to jail for debt. They were selfish, superstitious, and bigoted in the extreme. They came over here to get a chance. The real American was the Indian, and they solved that problem by killing him. The land was occupied, but they took it, and then our Puritan fathers proceeded to pass the most outrageous laws that any country ever knew anything about . . . .

We are told that the laboring man is against immigration. I don't know what he is for and against this year, and he doesn't know what he is for and against next year. I have always been for the poor man, but I am not for injustice as I see it either for the rich man or the poor man. Who are these working men? Most of them haven't been here as long as I have. I have been here so long that I don't need to work . . . .

We are told that we must not have Sicilians here because they are people who rob the rich; well, I should worry. Where do you suppose these rich people get all the money they are getting robbed of? The reason for this is that a few of them think they own America and they want to reduce the people to slavery, and they are doing it almighty fast. They are doing it while they talk of elections and fake prosperity. It is only people who have had prosperity who are prosperous. They own all the mines, all the coal, all the lumber, and everything else that is worth owning. They will soon own all the stores and the little corner storekeeper can go and tramp the streets, and I wouldn't care much, for they have always been fooled by the very people who are now trying to get their property away from them . . . .

This whole movement is narrow, stupid, mean, contemptible. I can, I believe, point out a few broad principles that should affect human beings. We have wandered from the ideas of the past; we used to encourage people to come here. The only habit or custom they have that is different from ours is that they take a drink of wine in the open, whereas we have to hide to drink ours. I have traveled quite extensively abroad and some in America, though I prefer to travel in Europe because of the present drought in America. Of course, Canada will do . . . .

When you try to interfere with the working out of the laws of nature, you get hurt, and for our puny minds to say that this is good and that is bad, and that this is better and that is worse for the short time we shall be here on earth is just foolishness.

Bibliographic Essay

The rhetorical environment of the 1920s in which Clarence Darrow lived and worked is best described in five major books. Roderick Nash's *The Nervous Generation: American Thought, 1917-1930* (Chicago: Rand McNally and Company, 1970) provides an excellent overview of the stresses and strains that caused considerable social ferment throughout the decade. Unlike the simplistic view presented by Frederick Lewis Allen in *Only Yesterday* (New York: Harper and Brothers, 1931) and Mark Sullivan in *Our Times: The United States, 1900-1925* (New York: Charles Scribner's Sons, 1935), Nash's work shows the 1920s to be an era of turmoil and self-doubt, brought on by the consequences of the First World War, increased urbanization and technological advance, racial and ethnic unrest, and many other factors. Nash's concept of social "nervousness" is the central conponent in the understanding of the so-called "Lost Generation."

Four other works should be consulted to draw realistic parameters around the 1920s. Clarke A. Chambers' *Seedtime of Reform–American Social Service and Social Action, 1918-1933* (Minneapolis, Minnesota: University of Minnesota Press, 1963) documents the many social relief programs that existed during this pre-New Deal period, exploding the myth that social ills were buried under the revelry of the Roaring Twenties. Don S. Kirschner's *City and Country–Rural Responses to Urbanization in the 1920s* (Westport, Connecticut: Greenwood Publishing Corporation, 1970) provides the specific analysis concerning the urban-rural split of philosophies that so marked the decade and had great impact upon the national issues of prohibition and immigration. William Preston's *Aliens and Dissenters–Federal Suppression of Radicals, 1903-1933* (Cambridge, Massachusetts: Harvard University Press, 1963) presents an excellent analysis of the immigration problem, while Andrew Sinclair's *Prohibition: The Era of Excess* (Boston: Little, Brown and Company, 1962) critically examines the stormy history of national Prohibition.

To understand the nature of Clarence Darrow, it is imperative that a wide array of sources be consulted. Four of Darrow's own writings provide insights into his attitudes, beliefs, and personality. His autobiography, *The Story of My Life* (New York: Grosset and Dunlap, 1932), gives Darrow's views on the important events in his life, explaining his philosophy of life and his compelling concern for the rest of humanity. Further insights are found by reading three of Darrow's periodical publications: "The Ordeal of Prohibition" (*The American Mercury*, II, August, 1924, pp. 419-427); "Is Man Fundamentally Dishonest?" (*Forum*, LXXVIII, December, 1927, pp. 884-889); and "The Futility of the Death Penalty" (*Forum*, LXXX, September, 1928, pp. 327-332). Two other works to be consulted to complete Darrow's personality profile were written by men who knew him very well. Arthur Garfield Hays, an outstanding attorney and, with Darrow, a member of the John T. Scopes defense team, provided personal observations and recollections in *Let Freedom Ring* (New York: Boni and Liveright, 1928). George G. Whitehead, Darrow's debate tour manager for the Redpath Lyceum Bureau, offered an up-close analysis of his client in *Clarence Darrow–The Big Minority Man* (Girard, Kansas: Haldeman-Julius Company, 1929).

The best secondary source of biographical/personality material is Irving Stone's *Clarence Darrow for the Defense* (Garden City, New York: Doubleday and Company, Inc., 1941), an exhaustive cradle-to-grave portrait of Darrow. Similar in scope, but not as thoroughly researched, is Miriam Gurko's *Clarence Darrow* (New York: Thomas Y. Crowell Company, 1965). Gurko's work, however, makes for more pleasurable reading than does the volume by Stone.

One other book should be consulted because of its intellectual approach to the study of Darrow: *Clarence Darrow and the American Literary Tradition* (Cleveland, Ohio: Western Reserve University Press, 1962) by Abe C. Ravitz. Short-length analyses of lesser value are provided by Francis X. Busch, *Prisoners at the Bar* (New York: Bobbs-Merrill Company, 1952); Alan Hynd, *Defenders of the Damned* (New York: A. S. Barnes and Company, 1960); and William M. Kunstler, *The Case for Courage* (New York: William Morrow and Company, 1962).

Finally, to study other writers' viewpoints concerning Darrow's rhetorical skills, three works should be consulted: (1) Martin H. Maloney's chapter in *A History and Criticism of American Public Address*, volume three, edited by Marie K. Hochmuth (New York: Longmans, Green and Company, 1955); (2) Maloney's "The Forensic Speaking of Clarence Darrow" (*Speech Monographs*, XIV, 1947, pp. 111-126); and (3) Horace G. Rahskopf's chapter in *American Public Address*, edited by Loren Reid (Columbia, Missouri: University of Missouri Press, 1961). Besides these published works, a number of unpublished graduate theses and dissertations have concentrated upon Darrow's speaking skills and activities. Three such works are recommended for study: (1) Harry W. Greene's "The Debates and Religious Forums of Clarence Darrow" (Master's thesis, Northern Illinois University, 1970); (2) John B. Roberts' "The Speech Philosophy of Clarence Darrow" (Master's thesis, State University of Iowa, 1941); and (3) Akira Sanbonmatsu's "Adaptation and Debate Strategies in the Speaking of Clarence Darrow and Alexander Rorke in *New York vs. Gitlow*" (Ph.D. dissertation, Pennsylvania State University, 1968).